BACKGAMMON
The Quick Course to Winning Play

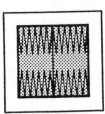

BACKGAMMON
The Quick Course to Winning Play

 by DON STERN

GALAHAD BOOKS • NEW YORK CITY

Contents

For Caryn, who cheerfully tested my theories
and rolled well—too well—at crucial times.

My thanks to
My wife, Carol, who encouraged me, helped type
the manuscript, reviewed it, and offered constructive
criticism . . . and gave me the pocket calculator on
which I figured the odds.

The Columbia Scientific Company, for manufacturing a
reliable and practical pocket calculator accurate
to nine places.

Lynn Sonberg, whose suggestions and publishing
acumen made this a better book.

And to Irving Woods, David Paul, and
Gordon Draper.

Introduction

Backgammon is a game of paradoxes. Called the "King of Games," it has been for almost its entire 5,000-year history also the "Game of Kings," played by monarchs, nobles, and the idle rich. Yet the backgammon board of twelve slim triangles of alternating colors on each side is now familiar to almost all Americans from every walk of life, for it was on the back of the folding checkerboard of their youth. As children, we all occasionally played the game and a vague recollection of the rules is still lodged somewhere in the recesses of our minds.

On the surface, backgammon is a game of chance played with dice. The rankest tyro can win a game, even a short match, against the greatest expert. But the luck of the roll evens out and in the long run the expert invariably triumphs. Still, there are a handful of men who regularly lose $100,000 a year at backgammon but feel certain that eventually their "luck" must turn.

The rules of the game are so simple that they can be learned in one sitting. The intricacies of strategy, position, and timing, however, would challenge the capabilities of even the most sophisticated computer.

Children enjoy backgammon, adults find it a pleasant social diversion, it is adaptable to many forms of tournament play, and is probably the finest gambling game devised by man.

Perhaps the greatest paradox of all is backgammon's emergence after five centuries as the most popular game craze of the 1970s. Not since the early days of contract bridge has any game caught the public mood so quickly and irresistibly.

Intrinsically, backgammon is indeed beautifully constructed. No two backgammon games can be identical; ties are impossible; games are fast (averaging less than ten minutes in tournaments); luck and skill mix inexorably in the play so that one lucky roll can destroy an apparently impregnable position. The excitement of handling the dice, the expectation of a favorable roll, the uncertain and sudden changes of fortune, all keep the players on edge and totally engrossed. The fever generated by a game of backgammon can best be compared to the tenseness of craps or poker. It is just as unpredictable and nerve-wracking, but backgammon is also subtle, strategic, and psychological, and affects the true *aficionado* like a narcotic.

Backgammon can be played anywhere, any time, for most boards are compact and portable and the game is designed for two players (more can play in the form known as chouette). Like most classic games, backgammon is warfare in microcosm: two opposing armies clash, try to pass through each other's ranks to their objective, capturing enemy men along the way, setting up blockades against the other's progress. After each roll one must decide whether to attack, to defend, to retreat temporarily, to set a trap, to ambush, or to temporize. But unlike any other recognized game of skill, the captured pieces are not permanently removed from play, but are sent back to reenter the field at the furthest point from their homeland, facing a long arduous journey. ("Back game" is the literal translation of the Middle English word back gamen.) One such "hit" or setback can cost the entire game. Yet, so subtle is the game, the captured piece enters the most vulnerable area of his opponent—the same quarter from which he must remove his men in order to gain victory. The alien men in this sensitive region threaten his victory when it is closest. Ironically, although the enemy's pieces cannot be permanently put out of play, one may deliberately remove his own, and this, in fact, is the objective of the game: he who removes all his pieces first wins.

These, tnen, are some of the features that have kept the game alive in elite circles for centuries. But to account for the current craze, we must go back to the 1920s, when some unheralded genius introduced the doubling cube. This simple device allows either player to double the stakes, but his opponent has the option of declining and forfeiting only the original stake. Paradoxically, it is equally correct for one player to offer a double and for the other to accept, though he knows he is behind.

The doubling cube introduced an exotic pattern into the game, for although either player may make the first double, the other then "controls the cube" and he alone can redouble. Expert games rarely go beyond one double and one redouble, but daredevils have been known to agree on automatic doubles or use the doubling cube so recklessly that they play out games of sixty-four times the original stake.

Doubling has its own contradictions: it is unwise to double when slightly ahead in the early game, for a modest shift in the dice rolls or position may elicit an unwelcome redouble. It may also be wrong to offer a double when one is far ahead, for the double will be flatly rejected, while the chance of winning a double stake can be preserved without the doubling cube: if one player removes all his pieces before his opponent has removed one of his, a "gammon" is scored, doubling the value of the game.

Just as a poker player may be intimidated by a large bet and wisely "fold" his hand, so the backgammon player must learn when to decline doubles. But unlike poker, there are no concealed hands, hence no chance to bluff. Yet the experienced backgammon player will soon discover the doubling threshold of a weaker opponent; if the latter trusts the expert unquestioningly, he will eventually decline doubles even though he has the superior game.

The doubling cube heightens the strategic and psychological elements of the game and constantly tests the mettle of the participants. Several times during a game they must ask themselves:

Should a double be offered, risking a turn for the worse and a devastating redouble? Will this particular opponent accept a double in this particular position? Should a proffered double be accepted, or is it better to forfeit the game and try to recoup the next—perhaps doubled and redoubled—game? To make the right decision most of the time demands concentration, keen awareness, and nerves of steel.

Bridge, too, has its doubles and redoubles, but once made, they must be accepted. Backgammon grants the option to accept or decline—and imposes an ordeal of decision.

The doubling cube is but one of the developments that led to backgammon's current popularity. Another is a daring change in strategy of recent vintage. Until recently, backgammon was regarded as basically a racing game: whoever rolled the better dice and was fortunate enough to escape capture would generally win. Only in the last ten years has it been demonstrated that near-hopeless positions can be overcome by keeping some men back, deliberately entrapped, until their time comes to strike and wrest victory from defeat.

As in a gambit in chess, the backgammon player may willingly sacrifice his pieces in order to establish a sounder overall position. As in bridge, he may cunningly time his plays so as to entrap or embarrass his opponent.

Timing thus became an exciting new dimension in the game. To slow up the march of his army, the expert player offers some of his men for capture, sometimes deliberately stringing them out so that his opponent cannot avoid hitting them. The time thus bought in bringing these men back into play and around to their home quarter permits the establishment of a strong position just at the time his opponent is forced to weaken his. Then, even a single capture could turn the tables and ensure victory.

This bold new approach truly revolutionized the game. One-sided games became a rarity. The better players abandoned the old style of playing safe in favor of taking risks early. The luck of the roll thus became secondary to the skill of the player.

The introduction of the doubling cube and of the aggressive new style alone would earn for backgammon its current wide acceptance. But other factors contributed. Science and technology have promoted a better understanding of game theory and probabilities among all players, but particularly among the inventive young Turks developing their new theories.

Since backgammon is open, aboveboard, and totally visible, it is a kibitzers' paradise. The onlooker sees no more and no less than the players; if he brashly second-guesses a play, it may annoy the players, but it has little effect on the game itself, for that move is done and a new position arrives after the next player rolls.

That artists have portrayed backgammon games since ancient times is evidence of the game's enduring popularity, providing a rich heritage of backgammon paintings and prints throughout history. Interestingly, almost all show not only two players in combat but also a circle of absorbed onlookers. Even today, there are many who relish the game vicariously from the sidelines but do not trust their gambling prowess sufficiently to play at the going stakes.

It is our view, perhaps prejudiced, that backgammon combines the best of all classic intellectual games. The betting aspect of poker and the sacrificial gambits in chess have been mentioned. The analogy to bridge is particularly apt, for many of today's backgammon champions are also bridge experts. They, better than most, can appreciate the boldness in play, nuances in timing, taking of calculated risks to reap the greater reward, creation of positional coups. There is an element of luck in both games, but in bridge it is minimal after the cards are dealt. In backgammon, on the other hand, the uncertainty of chance persists until the last roll.

Both in backgammon and the complex Japanese game of Go, beginners delight in capturing the opposing pieces and thereby misread the purpose of the game. In backgammon, the objective is to bring one's pieces safely around the board and "bear them off"; in Go, the winner is the one who surrounds or controls the most territory. But the temptation to hit the adversary's pieces and the close decisions whether to do so add to the zest of both games.

Like the craps player, the backgammon players must have an understanding of the probabilities of the rolls of the dice. Even here, however, backgammon is subtler. The craps player is concerned with only the total of the two dice. There are thirty-six combinations that produce eleven totals, but these can be simply graphed on a regular curve: one combination for 2 or 12; two for 3 and 11; three for 4 and 10; and so on until the six maxmimum possibilities for a 7.

In backgammon there are seventeen ways to realize a 6, but only six to get a 7. This oddity comes about because the backgammon player recognizes three separate values with each roll of the dice—each die separately and the total of the two dice. Moreover, the consequences of any roll vary with the disposition of the opponent's men. As if this were not enough, doubles in backgammon count for twice their value at craps—and hence have *four* values—which invalidates the probability table so familiar to the craps player.

With all its obvious advantages, backgammon has a bright present and a promising future. Whether it will ever overtake bridge as America's favorite intellectual game is a matter of conjecture, but certain parallels should be noted. Bridge began to prosper when a single set of laws was promulgated by a group of leading players. Similarly in 1931, backgammon's laws were resolved in a meeting of representatives of leading clubs and these laws have largely met the test of time. Bridge flourished through well-publicized money challenges and tournaments. Backgammon tournaments offer even larger financial rewards. Prince Alexis Obolensky organized the first international backgammon tournament in the early 1960s, and they have been held annually since with larger attendance and more publicity. Tournaments have sprung up all over the country and private backgammon clubs are being formed at a rapid clip. In 1972, the Backgammon Association of America was founded to update the rules, to organize playoffs for national tournaments, and, ultimately, to certify experts by awarding victory points. This is virtually the same route bridge traveled with the formation and growth of the American Contract Bridge League.

In both fields social games at home far outnumber formal tournaments. (There are some 200,000 members of the American Contract Bridge League, but an estimated 30 million social bridge players in this country.) Since it takes but two to play backgammon and a backgammon game can be held anywhere, it is not as remote as it may seem to envision the day when backgammon may inherit the mantle that bridge has worn so long.

For this royal game to survive fifty centuries and then to surge forth as the leading intellectual game would be the greatest paradox of all—or perhaps more puzzling is the wisdom of the ancients in maintaining the game through the ages without the advantages of a doubling cube, a codified set of rules, exciting new tactical ideas, or organizational support. But grateful we should be, for we are now given the purest and the simplest, the most complex and the subtlest game known to man.

HOW TO USE THIS BOOK

This book aims to develop a true understanding and appreciation of backgammon and to convey the basic concepts and strategies of winning play. Step by step, it will show the reasons for various moves so that the beginner may progress rapidly to higher levels.

PRACTI-GAMMON®, a backgammon board with extra men, has been constructed on the inside back cover. It folds out so that it is completely visible and playable while you are reading this book. Be sure to make the moves on this board as they are explained in the book, because visualizing moves can never take the place of actually moving the pieces.

The board should also be used in answering the quizzes to help reinforce the winning pointers and start you playing on your own that much sooner.

Of course, if you have a full-size backgammon set beside you as you read this book, so much the better. What really counts is that you play out the recommended moves and make your own decisions on the others.

The sooner you play against real opponents, the sooner your game will improve. Try to play against many opponents, for you can learn from the great diversity in styles and strategies you will encounter. Play in tournaments and seek out better players in friendly or small-stake games (else the education prove too costly), but do not expect your opponents to evaluate your game or give pointers.

This book will start you on your way to becoming a winner by showing you the tactics, strategy, psychology, and attitude that are the mark of the winning player.

What this book—or any book—*cannot do* is to elevate the amateur to expert rank, for the expert's gifts cannot be easily taught: a finely honed gambling instinct, a keen psychological sense, a mastery of the laws of probabilities, supreme confidence and coolness under fire, the experience gained from thousands of games against his peers. The backgammon professional has a feel for the game, loves it, and gives it all his energy.

No, this book will not make you an expert, only a winner in the amateur league. One section of the final chapter, however, may save you a considerable amount of money; it gives clues for recognizing the hustler, so that you are less likely to be beguiled into a one-sided, high-stakes game. Perhaps that will prove to be the winningest tip of all.

CHAPTER I
Equipment, Rules, & Etiquette

The rules of backgammon are simple and can be mastered with little study.

EQUIPMENT

- **Thirty checkers,** or *men* (terms defined in the glossary will be printed in italics the first time they appear in the text), divided into two groups of fifteen each. Each group is distinguished by its own color. The most popular color combinations are black and white, red and white, and red and black. The men are placed on:

- **A backgammon board** (Figure 1), consisting of twenty-four narrow triangles, called *points,* that face toward the center of the board. There are twelve points on each side of the board. Each one lines up with a corresponding point on the opposite side to produce a symmetrical arrangement.

    The points alternate in color to help the players calculate their moves quickly. Sometimes the color of the points matches the color of one player's men. This has no significance in the play; it definitely does *not* mean that these points belong to that player in any fashion.

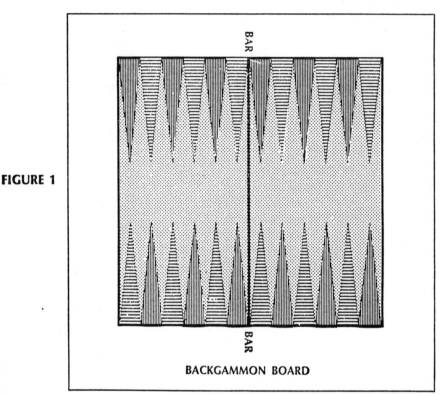

FIGURE 1

BAR

BAR

BACKGAMMON BOARD

Most backgammon boards are portable and are converted into a carrying case by folding along a hinged *bar* that runs along the midpoint of the board in the same direction as the points. On these sets both the bar and the perimeter of the board are raised, leaving the playing area recessed. Even on flat, stationary sets, there will be a strip indicating the bar, for the bar serves three purposes in the play: (1) it divides each player's side into his *home board* and his *outer board;* (2) like the alternating colors of the points, the bar aids the players to figure their moves rapidly; (3) it is the temporary resting place for men who have been *hit* and are waiting to reenter.

● **A pair of dice,** preferably two sets of different colors, so that each player may have his own and not have to exchange one set with every roll.

- **Two dice cups** (optional) with which to shake the dice. The dice could be shaken and rolled from one hand just as satisfactorily, but the sound of their rattling in a cup adds to the excitement and provides some insurance against a sharp gambler manipulating the dice.
- **A doubling cube,** generally larger than any of the dice, with the numbers 2, 4, 8, 16, 32, 64 on its six faces. A casual game can be played without a doubling cube, but it would lack one of the most fascinating and vexing elements of backgammon.

OBJECT OF THE GAME

To move all of one's men into one's home board and then to *bear* them *off* (remove them). The first player who bears off all his men wins the game.

PRELIMINARIES

The men are placed on the board as shown in Figure 2. Note that both the home boards and outer boards are opposite each other; therefore one player has his home table on his right, while the other, of necessity, has his home table on his left. By custom, the home tables face the source of light, but in practice, players must learn to play from either side of the table.

In Figure 2—but not on real backgammon sets—the points are numbered from 1 to 12 on each side of the board, starting at the point in the home board closest to the edge. This standard numbering system saves time in describing the moves and will be used in the figures and text through the book. Since there are two points for each number—always opposite each other—those on white's side will be designated by a "W" before the number (W1, W2, etc.) and those on black's side will have a "B" preceding the number (B1, B2, etc.). This prevents confusion and saves words in describing the moves.

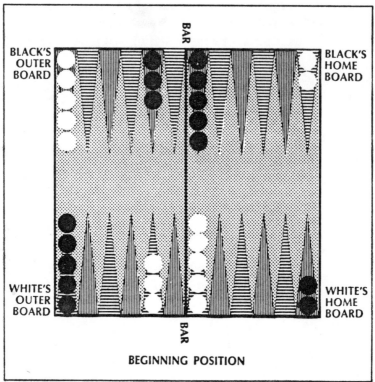

FIGURE 2

BEGINNING POSITION

Caution: This letter code *identifies the point, not the color of the men* who occupy it. Observe, for example, that in the original setup black men occupy points W1 and W12, while white men rest on B1 and B12.

Only one point has a special name in common use: the 7 point (both W7 and B7) is popularly known as the *bar point.* An easy way to remember this is that it is the closest unoccupied point to the bar in the beginning position.

Neither of the two seating arrangements described offers any real advantage, so generally the players simply sit down, set up the pieces, as in Figure 2, and start to play. But if there is a disagreement about seats, color, or dice, the players roll their dice and the one with the higher roll wins the decision.

To start the game proper after the men are set up in the starting position, each player rolls one die. The player with the higher roll goes first and takes as his first move the rolls of both dice, as if he had rolled both. For example, if you roll a 6 and your opponent rolls a 3, you move first and your first move consists of a 6 and a 3.

If the first roll is a double, the dice are rolled again—as often as necessary—until two different numbers turn up. Some people turn the doubling cube from 64—its original position—to 2, thus doubling the value of the game, when the first roll is a double. But this *automatic double* is not included in the rules of backgammon and should not be played, for it is a capricious way of giving a greater value to some games. However, if both players agree beforehand to play automatic doubles, it is perfectly proper.

After the first player makes his move, his opponent rolls both of his dice and moves accordingly. Thereafter, the two players alternate, rolling both dice each time.

DIRECTION OF MOVEMENT

The reader should imagine himself playing with white pieces with his home board to his right (W1 through W6), and the figures in this book and the PRACTI-GAMMON® board in the back of the book are so drawn. Black is the opponent; his home board is to his left (B1 through B6).

White—to repeat, the player with his home board to his right—moves his men counterclockwise: from his opponent's home board, then to his opponent's outer board (B7 through B12), then *turning the corner* into his own outer board (W7 through W12), and finally into his own home board. Black—playing his home board to his left—moves in the opposite direction, clockwise, but the progression is the same: from his opponent's home board to his opponent's outer board, then to his outer board, then to his home board. Figure 3 shows the direction of movement for both players.

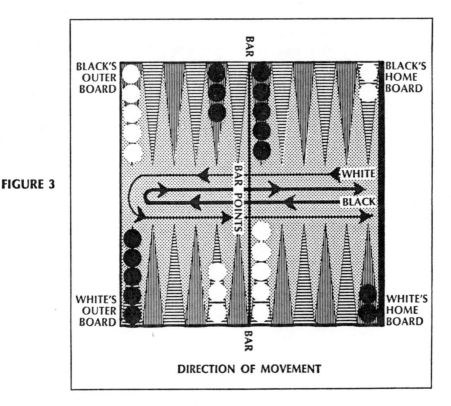

FIGURE 3

DIRECTION OF MOVEMENT

The movement for either player resembles a C, a horseshoe, or three-quarters of a circle. But the circle cannot be completed, for there is no direct move from W1 to B1 or *vice versa*. To illustrate this barrier, a solid line has been drawn in Figure 3, separating the two home boards. This, of course, does not appear on real backgammon sets, nor on the later figures in this book, for it would unnecessarily clutter up the board.

MECHANICS OF MOVING

The men are advanced on the board in their proper direction according to the rolls of the die. Each pip on a dice is equivalent to 1 point on the board. Thus a roll of 5 on one die advances

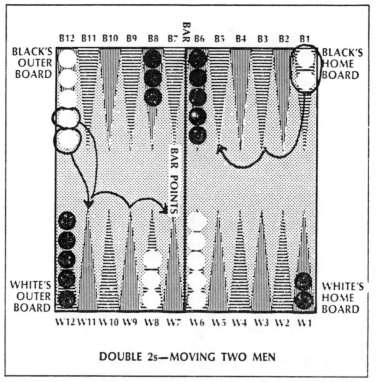

FIGURE 4

DOUBLE 2s—MOVING TWO MEN

one man by 5 points. However, each die is considered a separate move. For example, if the second die shows a 3, for a total roll of 5-3, a second man can be moved 3 points, or the first man may be advanced 3 points further, for a total move of 8. In the latter case, the man must *touch down* on a playable point after making his 5 move. The player determines the order he wishes to take his moves—5 then 3, or 3 then 5, and this option can be important, as will be shown in the next section.

A player must move according to the rolls on both dice, if he can legally do so. He cannot waive the roll of one die or his entire move, even though all his possible moves are hazardous. In the rare case where a player can legally move one, but not both of his rolls, he must move the larger one.

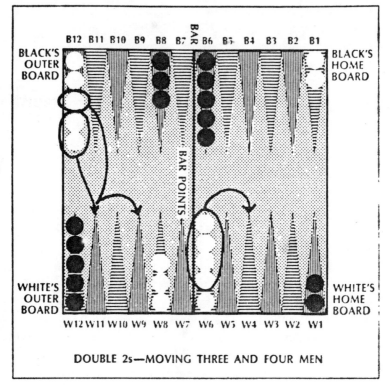

FIGURE 5

DOUBLE 2s—MOVING THREE AND FOUR MEN

DOUBLES

Doubles, in backgammon, have a special value. They count as if four dice with the same numeral had been thrown. Thus double 2s count as 2-2-2-2—four moves of 2 each, for a total of 8. Four different men may each be moved 2 points, or one may be advanced the full 8 points. In between, there are three other options: move one man 2 points and another 6; move two men 4 spaces each, move one man 4 points and two others 2 points each. In other words, the four moves of a double may be apportioned among one, two, three, or four men. But each of the four moves must terminate or touch down on a legally playable point.

All told, there are ninety-three different combinations for moving double 2s. To show them all would confuse rather than clarify. Therefore we will simply show one example of each type of move (please refer to Figures 4 and 5).

Lest you conclude that the entire move must emanate from the same point, Figure 6 shows four men moving off four different points. It is equally permissible to move men from three different points or two.

The peculiar rule for doubles would bewilder the craps player, for in backgammon it is possible to have moves of 15, 16, 18, 20, and 24. (Four 4s count to 16, four 5s to 20, four 6s to 24; if one man is moved the value of three numbers, then three 5s total 15 and three 6s account for a move of 18.)

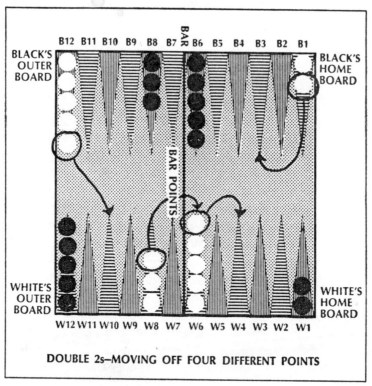

FIGURE 6

DOUBLE 2s—MOVING OFF FOUR DIFFERENT POINTS

SHORTCUTS TO COUNTING MOVES

- An even-numbered move—2, 4, 6, etc.—lands on a point of the same color as the starting point. Try it on the PRACTI-GAMMON board in the back.
- An odd-numbered move lands on a point of the opposite color.
- A move of 6 comes to rest at a point of the same color and same relative position in the next board. For example, to move a white man on B1 6 spaces without counting, you note that he now occupies a black point farthest from the next board (black's outer board). His new position therefore will be at B7, the black point distant from your outer board. Of course, it is easier to compute with the point numbers—B1 + 6 = B7—when studying the illustrations in this book and the game board in back. But that will prove to be a lazy habit when you play against an opponent on an unnumbered full-size set.

In turning the corner—going from black's outer board to your own—you must adjust for the change in direction and numbering sequence. For example, in black's outer board B12 is the nearest white point in the *direction in which you are moving*, so a move of 6 lands on W7, the closest white point in your outer board.

You will go wrong if you identify the points by right and left: B12 is the furthest white point on your left in black's outer board; so is W11 in yours, but the journey from B12 to W11 is but 2 spaces.

This shortcut also works for the four interior points in each board. It may sound complicated on paper, but after a few tries in moving the men it will become second nature. Then you can abandon the painstaking task of counting each pip on the dice as you move and more quickly figure where each possible move ends and whether you want to make that particular journey.

PLAYABLE MOVES

A man may touch down (in transit between two or more moves of the same roll) or stop on any point that is (1) unoccupied by any men, (2) occupied by one or more of his own men, or (3) occupied by one opposing man.

It is not permissible for you and your opponent to have men on the same point, so in case (3), when you touch down or stop at a point occupied by one opposing man, that man is *hit* and sent to the bar, whence he must reenter at his opponent's home board. Thus a single man on a point is vulnerable to capture, and is appropriately termed a *blot*.

However, a point while occupied by two or more men is

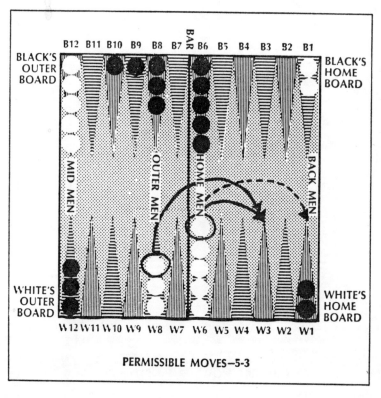

FIGURE 7

PERMISSIBLE MOVES—5-3

invulnerable to attack and is therefore known as a *blocked point.* A great deal of backgammon strategy revolves around *making a point*—bringing two men of the same color together on the same point, so that it becomes a blocked point. This not only safeguards both men from capture, but also denies that point to your opponent as he attempts to bring his men into his home board.

Figure 7 will help clarify permissible and prohibited moves. Note first that we have assigned names to the four clusters of men in the starting position. The *back men* are so called because they are the furthest back and have the longest way to travel before reaching the home board. Similarly, the *home men* are already in the home board, the *outer men* are nearby, in the

FIGURE 8

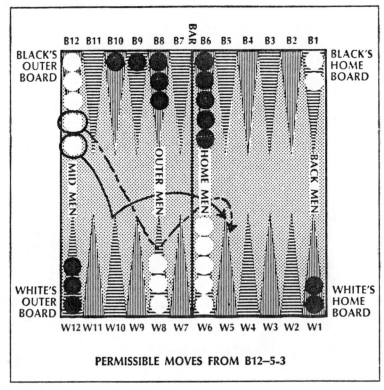

PERMISSIBLE MOVES FROM B12–5-3

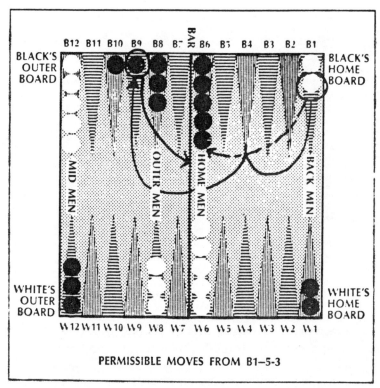

FIGURE 9

PERMISSIBLE MOVES FROM B1—5-3

outer board, and the *mid men* (in the opponent's outer board) are midway home.*

Figure 7 shows the position after you rolled a 3 and your opponent rolled a 4 to start the game. He used his 4-3 roll to move two of his mid men, one to B10, the other to B9. You, white, now roll a 5-3. You cannot move a home man 5 points to W1, for that would put him on black's blocked point—an illegal move.

You can move a home man 3 points—to W3—for that is un-occupied, and then make a point by moving an outer man 5

---

* Back man is a well-established backgammon term, but the other three have been coined by the author to aid in the explanations.

spaces to join them on W3. This move is also shown on Figure 7.

Another possibility is to move a mid man the full 8 points to W5, which would leave a blot (Figure 8). In this case, he would touch down on W10—unoccupied—or W8—occupied by your men—either of which is permissible.

A third possibility is to move a back man the full roll to hit the blot on B9. So you count out 5 points, only to find that you have landed on black's blocked point at B6, an illegal move. Is there another way? Yes, move the 3 first to B4, which is un-occupied, and then count off 5 spaces to hit black on B9. That is shown on Figure 9 and black's man is *sent to the bar.*

COMING OFF THE BAR

When a player has a man on the bar, his first duty is to bring that man off the bar and back into play. He can make no other move before that. It is helpful in visualizing the position if we mentally move the bar off the set and place it alongside the two home boards (Figure 10). The man on the bar—black, in this ex-ample—should be imagined as starting off outside the playing area at *point zero,* forced to reenter in his opponent's (white's) home board. Except for that restriction, he moves exactly as described earlier: he may stop on any unoccupied point, his own or his opponent's blot, or on his own blocked point. He cannot come in on his opponent's blocked point. If he hits an opposing blot, he sends that man to the bar and the same procedure applies to his reentry. He, too, must start his journey from the opponent's home board.

In actual play it is easier to check whether the count on either die matches up with any point on the opponent's home board that is not blocked by him. If so, the man on the bar may reen-ter at that point. In Figure 10, for example, if black rolls a 4-3, he can bring his man in on either W4 or W3, as both are unoc-cupied. He can use the second half of his roll to bring that man out of white's bar point (W7), or to move another man. If black had instead rolled a 5-1, he could come out on either the W5 or W1, since W5 is vacant and W1 is occupied by black's men. However, he could not then move his man the second half of the roll, for that would put him on white's blocked point at W6.

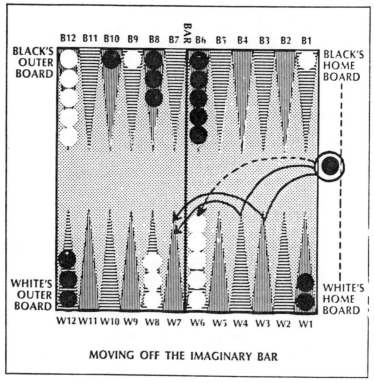

FIGURE 10

MOVING OFF THE IMAGINARY BAR

Nor can black come out directly onto W6. If black rolls a 6 on one die, he is forced to use the number on his other die to bring his man out. And if black rolls double 6s, ordinarily an excellent roll, he cannot come out at all and would forfeit his move. Remember, a player can make no other move while he has a man on the bar.

Let's take a more complicated position to illustrate the possibilities: Figure 11. The table on page 32 lists all twenty-one possible rolls.*

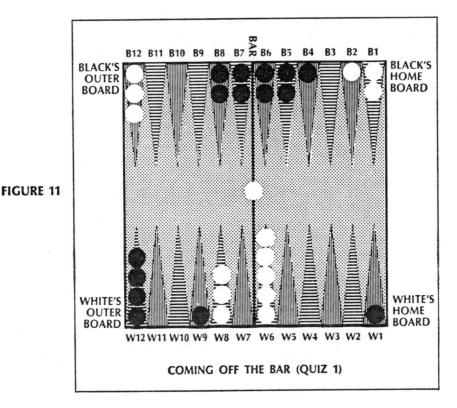

FIGURE 11

COMING OFF THE BAR (QUIZ 1)

Decide for yourself which rolls permit the white man on the bar to reenter and which do not. Then judge which rolls bring the man in on a *free move*—permitting two points of reentry— and which are *forced moves*—allowing only one point of entry.

---

* There are actually thirty-six possible rolls, but thirty of them—all but the doubles—count as only fifteen combinations for this purpose, as there are fifteen duplications. For example, 6-5 and 5-6 are two separate possibilities, but count as only one combination, since a player has the option of deciding in which sequence they should be played.

Lastly, decide which moves can hit an enemy blot, which can make a point—where white had only one man previously—and which would put a man onto a vacant point.

The table on page 32 has columns for each category, on which the reader can put either a check mark or a point number, as indicated. Remember you are white reentering on black's home board. Consider all possibilities. There are some surprises, such as five entries each for the rolls of 3-1, 2-1, and the double 1s.

Frequently, alas, you may find yourself with two—or more—men on the bar. You must get them all onto the opponent's home board before you can make any other play.

In Figure 12, white can bring in both of his men with any of nine rolls—out of a total of thirty-six. Thus, the odds are 3 to 1

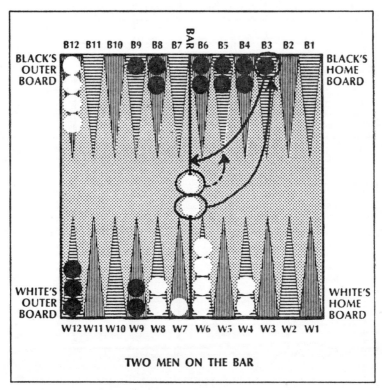

FIGURE 12

TWO MEN ON THE BAR

QUIZ 1
WHITE COMING OFF THE BAR IN FIGURE 11

Roll of dice	Cannot reenter ✓	Free move can enter on: and:		Forced move, can re-enter only on	Hits black's blot on:	Rein-forces white's blocked point on:	Makes a blocked point on:	Lands on vacant space on:
6-6								
6-5								
6-4								
6-3								
6-2								
6-1								
5-5								
5-4								
5-3								
5-2								
5-1								
4-4								
4-3								
4-2								
4-1								
3-3								
3-2								
3-1								
2-2								
2-1								
1-1								

Now check your answers against the following table.

ANSWERS TO QUIZ 1
WHITE COMING OFF THE BAR IN FIGURE 11

Roll of dice	Cannot reenter	Free move Can enter on: and:		Forced move, can re-enter only on:	Hits black's blot on:	Rein-forces white's blocked point on:	Makes a blocked point on:	Lands on vacant space on:
6-6	✓							
6-5	✓							
6-4				B 4	B 4			
6-3				B 3				B 3
6-2				B 2			B 2	
6-1				B 1		B 1		
5-5	✓							
5-4				B 4	B 4			
5-3				B 3				B 3
5-2				B 2			B 2	
5-1				B 1		B 1		
4-4				B 4	B 4			
4-3		B 4	B 3		B 4			B 3
4-2		B 4	B 2		B 4		B 2	
4-1		B 4	B 1		B 4	B 1		
3-3				B 3				B 3
3-2		B 3	B 2				B 2	B 3
3-1		B 3	B 1		B 4*	B 1		B 3
2-2				B 2	B 4*		B 2	
2-1		B 2	B 1			B 1	B 2	B 3*
1-1				B 1	B 4*	B 1	B 2*	B 3*

* These moves are possible by advancing the man on the bar after he lands in black's home board.

against their reentry on the next roll. Let's assume that white rolls a 5-3. He brings in one man on B3, hitting the blot there and sending that man to the bar. But he cannot bring his second man out with the 5, since black has B5 blocked. So one white man stays on the bar, and a black man joins him there. This is the one situation where both players may have a man on the bar at the same time.

BEARING OFF

When all of one's men arrive in their home board, they can be removed according to the numbers rolled on the dice. This is called bearing off. A man may be borne off from any point

FIGURE 13

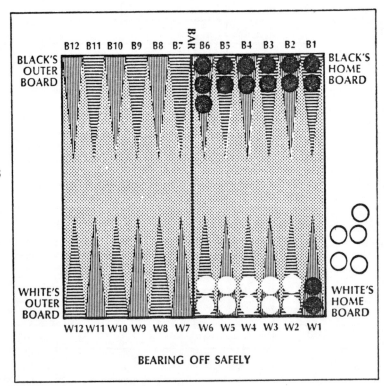

BEARING OFF SAFELY

corresponding to the number on the dice. A roll of 6 enables a man to be borne off from the 6 point. Visualize counting 6 points and you will see that this brings the man off the board. A 6-3 roll permits you to remove one man from the 6 point and one from the 3 point.

All too often, unfortunately, as you are bearing off your men, you leave a blot that is hit by one of your opponent's back men, which he has kept there for just that mission. Your man must of course reenter the playing area at your opponent's home board and be brought around to your home board. Until he arrives, you cannot bear off any additional men.

Naturally, you want to avoid leaving blots in the end game. You can by making alternate moves within your home board. In Figure 13, you have borne off five men and now roll a 4-2. It would be foolish to bear off one man each from W4 and W2, for that would leave two blots—on W4 and W2. Now a hit by black would probably cost you the game. Far better to move the two men on W6, one to W4, the other to W2, leaving no blots at all. If you had *three* men on your 6 point, you could safely bear off one of them by moving first to W4 (or W2) and then off the board.

Suppose you roll a 6 but have no men left on your 6 point. You are then permitted to bear off a man from W5, or from the highest point on which you have men remaining. But you cannot make this surrogate move if it is possible to move a man within your home board. Contrast white's and black's positions in Figure 14. If white rolls a 4, 5, or 6, he can remove a man from W3. But if black rolls a 5 or 4, he cannot remove any man, for he is first required to move his men from B6, as they constitute valid *interior moves* within his home board.

Just as in moving the pieces on the board and in coming in off the bar, the players decide which of their two rolls they wish to move first. It need not be the most economical. In Figure 15, you roll a 6-1. If you move your 6 first, removing the man on your W6 perforce, you will have to leave a blot when you

FIGURE 14

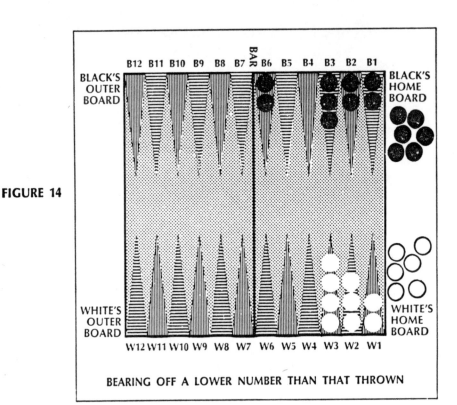

BEARING OFF A LOWER NUMBER THAN THAT THROWN

FIGURE 15

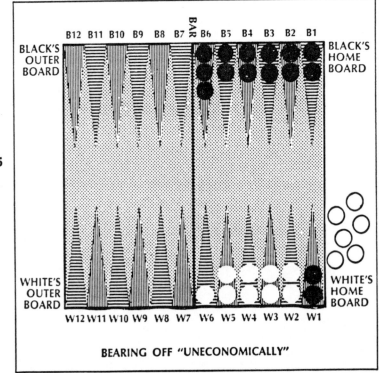

BEARING OFF "UNECONOMICALLY"

move a 1 from one of your blocked points. The safe but un-economical move is to advance the man on W6 by 1 point and then remove him. This is permissible, since you can no longer move a man 6 spaces within your home board. Now your blocked points remain intact and no blot is left.

VALUE OF THE GAME

The first player to bear off all his men wins the game. Usually his opponent will have borne off at least one man, and this con-stitutes a simple win—counting 1 unit toward the required total in a tournament or 1 unit at the agreed stake in a gambling game.

When the opponent has not been able to bear off even a single man, the victory is known as a *gammon* and is worth 2 units.* The highest value occurs when the opponent has, as be-fore, failed to bear off a single man and has at least one man in his opponent's home board or on the bar. This is called a *back-gammon* and is worth 3 units.

Once a player has borne off a man, he cannot be gammoned or backgammoned, even though one of his men may later be hit and not return to his home board before the game is over.

THE DOUBLING CUBE

At the beginning of the game the doubling cube is turned so that the number 64 is face up. It is then placed on the edge of the set midway between the players. Either player, before his turn to roll, may offer to double the stakes by turning the cube so that the number 2 is face up, and then by placing the cube on the bar on the opponent's side. The opponent may accept the double simply by nodding his head or giving some verbal indication or by moving the cube still closer to him. Or he may refuse equally politely or through more colorful language or

* Some people, vaguely remembering the backgammon rules from their child-hood, are under the mistaken belief that to avoid a backgammon one must only bring in all his men to his home board.

even by upsetting the board (this is considered bad form, but it has been known to happen under great provocation).

If the double is accepted, the doubler rolls and the game continues on at twice the money stake in a gambling game or at 2 units in a tournament match. If the double is refused, the game ends immediately and the doubler is credited with a 1 unit victory.

After the initial double, the player who accepted it *controls the cube.* He, and only he, can offer a redouble—in the same fashion, but turning the cube so that the figure 4 faces up. Then the right to redouble reverts to the first doubler, and so on. It is possible, though rare, for the cube to go to 64. In short tournaments usually only one double and one redouble are permitted.

Of course, if neither player doubles, the game is worth just 1 unit, even though the cube shows 64. (If the opponents cannot agree on whether the cube has been turned six times or not at all, they should switch their modest talents to a simpler game.)

A gammon or backgammon doubles or triples the value of the doubling cube. Thus a gammon when the cube shows 4 is worth 8 points (4 on the cube times 2 for the gammon); a backgammon when the cube shows 8 is worth 24 points (8 on the cube times 3 for the backgammon).

ETIQUETTE
- Backgammon is most enjoyable when played quickly in relative silence.
- Moves should be made with just one hand, as moving two men at the same time can be confusing.
- Customarily, the opposing dice are thrown on opposite sides of the bar, to minimize the chance of a premature roll intermingling the dice. Usually the dice are thrown on the half of the board to a player's right. When that is a player's home table and after it becomes crowded with pieces, it is permissible to throw the dice in the other half of the set.

- Dice are *cocked* when they do not come to rest squarely within the playing area, that is, on the rim, the bar, or any of the men. Such a roll is invalid and the dice must be rolled again.
- A player may retract his move and make another before he starts to pick up his dice, which signifies the end of his move.
- If a player has made an incorrect or incomplete move and signified his move is ended, his opponent may allow the move to stand or require its correction or completion.
- It is improper to pick up one's dice before completing the move, since that removes the one certain means of resolving a disagreement about the roll. Therefore, the opponent, if he insists, is entitled to the benefit of the doubt, but a polite and just solution is to permit a reroll.
- If a player rolls prematurely—before his opponent has completed his move—the opponent may allow the roll to stand or disallow it. However, this option should be judiciously exercised.
- A player may concede the game when it is impossible—or even unlikely—for him to win, provided his opponent agrees, that is, discounts the chance of a gammon or backgammon.
- The players may agree to draw a game without completing it, or to settle a game prematurely at a lesser or greater value than that shown on the doubling cube. When the latter case occurs, it is generally because a gammon is theoretically possible.

QUESTIONS STUDENTS ASK

The first encounter with a new game may create some confusion. We have compiled a list of questions students have asked during the first lesson and are reprinting them here, with the answers of course, to ensure that you do not start out with any misconceptions:

1. *Is there any limit to the number of men that may occupy a single point?*
   None. Theoretically, fifteen could, but we have never seen more than eight. Incidentally, to make room, just stack the extra ones on top of the others.
2. *Can I go backward if I want to hit a man?*
   No, you cannot reverse direction for any reason.
3. *Can I put my white men on black points?*
   Yes, the colors of the points are for convenience in counting, and have no connection with the colors of the men that may occupy them.
4. *Can I use the count on the dice any way I want to? For example, if I roll a 6, can I break it up into a 5 and a 1?*
   No, each number on a die must be moved as an indivisible integer.
5. *I know I cannot land on a blocked point, where my opponent has two men. But can I pass over such a point?*
   Yes, the rules only prohibit landing directly on that point.
6. *I notice that when five men are on a point, you can hardly see the triangle. I am just wondering whether such a point counts in making my move, or do I forget about it when pacing out my move?*
   Every point, occupied or unoccupied, counts in moving your roll.
7. *What about the bar? Does that count as a point in making a move?*
   No, the bar just separates the four boards and is a temporary home for a man who is hit.
8. *Must I use my entire roll?*
   Yes, unless you cannot legally do so—when every move lands on an enemy blocked point, or when you have a man on the bar who cannot come in.

9. Can I move a man off the board if I want to?
   Only when all your men in are in your home board. Then you bear them off according to the numbers on the dice.
10. Can I move from my home board to my opponent's home board?
   No, the only journey you can make from your home board is off the board entirely in bearing off, or to the bar if hit.

Before leaving this chapter, try this provocative quiz, designed to promote a clearer understanding of hitting blots, permissible moves, and the play of doubles.

QUIZ 2

You, white, rolled a 3 and black rolled a 4. He moved two mid men B9 and B10 to produce the position shown in Figure 16:

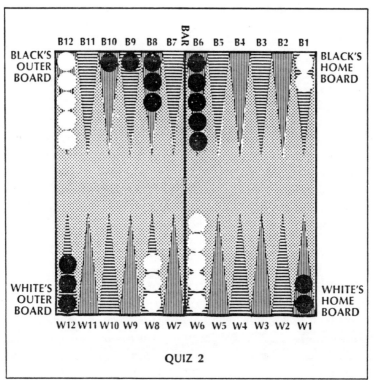

FIGURE 16

QUIZ 2

1. Which rolls allow you to hit the blot on
   a. B9?
   b. B10?
2. Are there any doubles that will not permit you to move one back man from B1:
   a. Even the number on one die?
   b. Twice the number on a die?
   c. Three times the number on a die?
   d. The full value of the double—four times the number on a die?
3. Is there any roll that permits you to put a back man into your outer board?
4. Is there any double you can play fully with one mid man at B12, moving him the total distance?
5. Now to your home man on W6. Are there any doubles you can play fully with one man?
6. Let's move more than one man off a point. Which doubles can you move entirely from the men on:
   a. B1?
   b. B12?
   c. W8?
   d. W6?

ANSWERS TO QUIZ 2

1. a. 6-2, 5-3 moving the 3 first, double 4s and double 2s hit the blot on B9.
   b. 6-3 and 5-4 (moving the 4 first) and double 3s hit the blot on B10.
2. a. Double 5s. The first 5 lands on B6, where black has a point.
   b. Besides double 5s, double 6s, for that puts down on W12, occupied by two black men.
   c. To double 5s and 6s, we must add double 4s. The third 4 sets down at W12.
   d. Double 3s will not go. The fourth 3 also counts out to W12. That leaves only double 1s and 2s fully playable from B1.
3. No. Of the doubles, the only ones you can move the full distance, double 1s and 2s, leave you short. The other doubles cannot get past W12, as we have just seen. And the largest roll of two different number is 6-5, which bring you out only to B12.

4. Only double 2s. Four of the doubles run into points owned by black: double 1s (the first 1 lands on W12), double 3s (the fourth 3 comes out on W1, as does the third 4 of double 4s and the second 6 of double 6s). Double 5s is disqualified for a different reason: the third 5 would bring a man off the board prematurely, that is before all of white's men are in his home board. The same objection would hold for double 6s and 4s, even if there were no adversely held point at W1.

5. Only double 1s. All the rest would send a man off the board illegally, since you have men outside your home table. There is a second bar to double 5s: the first 5 would land on W1, blocked by black.

6. a. All but double 5s and 6s. The various possibilities are:

   - Double 1s—single men to B2 and B4, or two men to B3.
   - Double 2s—single men to B3 and B7, or two men to B5.
   - Double 3s—to B4 and B10, or two men to B7.
   - Double 4s—two men to B9.

   b. All but double 1s. The others:

   - Double 6s—four men to W7.
   - Double 5s—four men to W8, or two men to W3, or two men to W8 and one to W3.
   - Double 4s—four men to W9, or two men to W5, or two men to W9 and one to W5.
   - Double 3s—four men to W10, or two men to W7, or two men to W10 and one to W7.
   - Double 2s—four men to W11, or two men to W9, or two men to W11 and one to W9, or one man to W11 and one to W7.

   c. • Double 3s, 2s, and 1s.
   - Double 3s—two men to W5 and one to W2, or two men to W2.
   - Double 2s—two men to W6 and one to W4, or two men to W4, or one man to W6 and another to W2.
   - Double 1s—two men to W7 and one to W6, or two men to W6, or one man to W7 and one to W5.

   d. • Double 4s, 3s, 2s, and 1s.
   - Double 4s—four men to W2.
   - Double 3s—four men to W3.

- *Double 2s—four men to W4, or two men to W4 and one to W2, or two men to W2.*
- *Double 1s—four men to W5, or two men to W5 and one to W4, or two men to W4, or one man to W5 and one to W3, or one man to W2.*

Whew! You will never have trouble moving doubles after this exercise. Now into the heart of the game.

CHAPTER II
Basic Strategy

A quick reading of the backgammon rules might persuade a beginner that winning strategy is largely a matter of avoiding leaving blots as the men are quickly moved around to the home board, where they can be borne off with dispatch. All told, the fifteen men must travel a total of 167 spaces, which could be accomplished in about twenty-one rolls (the average roll of the dice is 8 1/6). So, under this theory, whoever shoots luckier rolls figures to win.

The fallacy in this simplistic approach is that blots cannot be avoided. The odds against not being hit throughout an entire game are astronomical. Even if you were so fortunate to escape a hit, you still might lose the game. In Figure 17 you (white) have thirteen of your men in your home board, while black has brought but ten home. It is your roll and you are already 15 spaces ahead in the race. Yet your chances of winning the game are next to nil. That is because black has established a *prime*—six blocked points in a row—and until he is forced to *break his prime*—that is, move his men off one of those blocked points— white's back man cannot move. Even on a large roll like 6-5 or double 6s, white's back men have no permissible spot to touch down after the first roll.

All white can do is advance his other thirteen men further

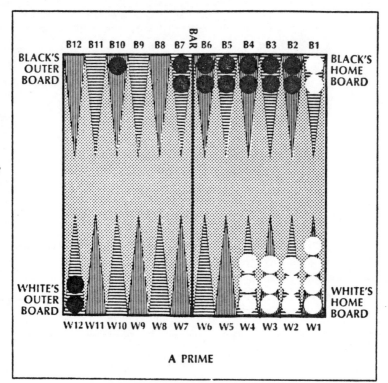

FIGURE 17

A PRIME

within his home board. After a few moves the situation may be as shown in Figure 18 with white to roll. Black has had to break his prime, but he has brought all his men in safely without leaving a blot. White meanwhile could not move his back men and has had to pile up the rest on W1, W2, and W3. Black is ready to bear off, but white cannot even start his back men home unless he rolls a 6. Double 6s would leave him just one roll behind. But the odds are 1,225 to 1 (35/1 x 35/1) against two successive double 6s, and that ignores black's chances to throw a double. More likely, white will throw just one 6 and be forced to move one of his back men prematurely, leaving the other vulnerable. (Remember a player cannot waive a roll if there is any way he can play it.) Now black can *point on the blot*—hit a blot while mak-

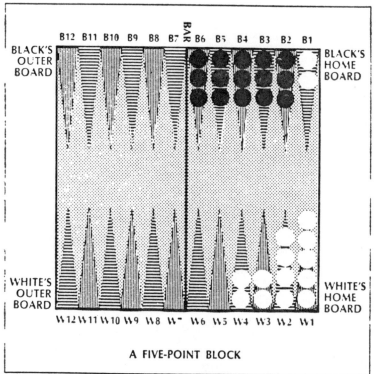

FIGURE 18

A FIVE-POINT BLOCK

ing a point there—with any of twenty-five rolls. Say black now rolls a 5-3. He moves one man from B6 to hit white's blot and covers this man with a man from B4. White's man is sent to the bar and we have Figure 19. Black has a *closed board*—a prime in his home board, and now white does lose his roll. For there is no roll that can bring in his man from the bar, and no other white man can be moved until he comes in. So white must wait until black leaves a blot or vacates one of the points in his home board. Only then can white roll again hoping to come in on an open point. White has virtually a hopeless game in this position.

How did white get into this predicament? Perhaps because he was overly concerned about exposing blot. Or he may have ignored the devastating effect of primes. For that matter, even

FIGURE 19

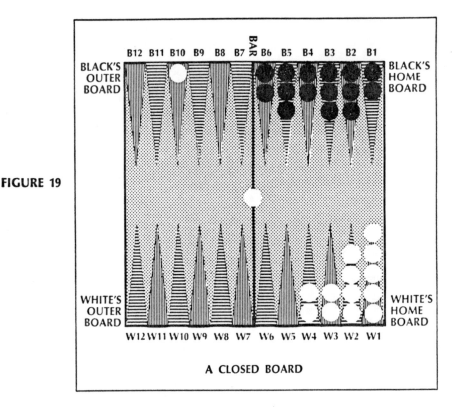

A CLOSED BOARD

three or four adverse blocked points can prevent a player from getting the full mileage from the rolls of his dice.

In short, there is much more to the game than the rules imply. The experienced player knows that blots are inevitable and he is not afraid of being hit. Realistically, he chooses to leave his blots early in the game in positions where they will help him build a strong blocking pattern in his outer and home boards or enable him to run with his back men. He does not worry when one of his blots is hit early, for that man can easily reenter the board with little lost. Later on, when three or more points in the opponent's home board are blocked, it may not be so easy. So one winning tactic is to take chances early in the game, rather than later.

This is where the beginner generally goes astray. Say he rolls a 4 and his opponent rolls a 1 to start the game. He must now play a 4-1 move and his fourteen choices: one of the mid or outer men can be moved the combined count of 5. (Note that the opponent's blocked point at B6 prevents a back man from moving 5 spaces; similarly, the men at B1 bar a home man from a 5 move.) The outer man can be moved 1 space or 4 spaces initially, but the mid man must take the 4 move first, as black has a blocked point one space away.

Or the roll can be played with two men from the same point —B1, W8, W6—or from two different points.

The beginner has no experience from which to choose among these fourteen options. Taking the simplistic view, he probably moves a mid man the combined count to W8, proudly announcing that he is "leaving no blots." True enough, but still a bad move.

THE EXPERT'S MOVE

The expert, on the other hand, automatically *splits* his back men—that is, moves one to B2—and brings a mid man to W9, deliberately leaving three unnecessary blots (Figure 20). Black can now hit one of these blots with any roll except 2-1—a 94% chance. It seems like an insane move, yet it is eminently correct, as we shall show.

This is still another of the paradoxes that abound in backgammon. The expert's move is based upon four separate reasons, each sound on its own merits:

(1) His opponent will gain no advantage from hitting one of the split back men, for it would advance his home men too far too early.

(2) Splitting the back men doubles their chances of hitting an opposing man who ventures into black's outer board.

(3) The blot on W9 is a *builder* who can assist in making a useful blocked point in white's outer or home board.

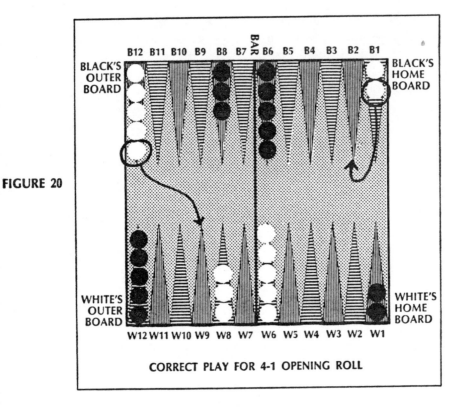

FIGURE 20

CORRECT PLAY FOR 4-1 OPENING ROLL

(4) The odds are five to one against the blot on W9 being hit.

Understanding the logic behind these four reasons will take the beginner a long way toward a good grasp of what backgammon is all about. So, we will take them one by one, but in reverse order:

(4) The odds are 5 to 1 against hitting the blot at W9. To hit that blot black must now roll an 8, else white will cover that blot on his next roll. There are six ways to get an 8 and all require counting both dice: 6-2, 2-6, 5-3, 3-5, double 4s and 2s. Since there are thirty-six possible rolls, the odds are 30 to 6 or 5 to 1 against the blot being hit.

All this may seem rudimentary to anybody who has ever handled dice before, but the dice seem to play tricks in backgammon. For instance, judge for yourself whether the odds are better or worse against rolling an 8, 7, or 6.

DIRECT AND COMBINATION SHOTS

The answers may surprise you: the odds against rolling a 7 are precisely the same as those against an 8—5 to 1. But there is almost an even chance—17 out of 36, to be precise—of rolling a 6. In short, there is a world of difference between leaving a blot 7 (or 8) spaces away and 6 spaces distant. The reason is simple enough: a 6 can be rolled with just one die—a *direct shot*—or as a total of both dice—a *combination shot*. Any number larger than 6 can be rolled only as a combination shot.

The full table of possibilities is given on page 54. It is not necessary to memorize it, but it is vital to grasp these principles:

- A hit from 6 or fewer spaces away is far more likely than one from 7 or more points distant. As a general rule, therefore, don't leave a blot open to a direct shot when you can instead leave one vulnerable only to a combined shot.
- If you must leave a blot open to a direct shot, the closer the better. There are just eleven ways* to hit a blot 1 point away, but seventeen ways to hit from 6 points away. The reason is that the smaller the number, the fewer combinations of two other numbers that will add to that number. As an extreme case, no two numbers combine for a total of 1, hence there are no combination shots for the number 1. But 5-1, 1-5, 4-2, 2-4, double 3s and 2s combine for a hit of 6.

* As previously pointed out, there are thirty-six possible rolls of two dice: 6 numbers on one die times 6 numbers on the other. But there are eleven ways in which a given number—1, in our example—can appear on either or both dice: double 1s, 6-1, 1-6, 5-1, 1-5, 4-1, 1-4, 3-1, 1-3, 2-1, 1-2. It may seem odd to count two possibilities for a roll like 6-1, but it checks out if you imagine throwing one green die and one red die. 6-1 can come up either as green 6-red 1 or red 6-green 1—two distinct possibilities. However, double 1s count for just

- In leaving a blot reachable by a combination shot, generally the farther away the better. There are some exceptions: combination shots of 7 and 8 are equally likely, as are 10 and 12, while 11 is riskier than 12.
- Any combination shot greater than 12 can be rolled by only one double, hence the odds are 35 to 1 against such a hit.

If you play enough backgammon you will become familiar with these probabilities. Until then, whenever the need arises, you can work out the odds on the spot and check them against the above table, which is reprinted on the PRACTI-GAMMON® board in back for convenience. You should not try to calculate the possibilities on every move, for it would slow down the game. But your game will improve if you can come up with an accurate count in a close, crucial situation.

The odds change when blocked points stand in the way. In Figure 21, for example, black can hit the blot on W9 in four ways—not six, as given in the table—since your point on W4 prohibits him from touching down on a 5-3 or 3-5 roll.

Incidentally, this position was reached as follows: white, 4-2, making his 4 point with one outer man and one home man (W8-W4, W6-W4). (Henceforth, we will use this shorthand system of notation: the first symbol indicating the point from which a man moves; the second indicating the point to which he is moved.) Black, 6-5, running a back man all the way to join his mid men (W1-W12). White, 4-1, moving a mid man to the 9 point (B12-W9) and splitting his back men (B1-B2).

---

one possibility: green 1-red 1 is identical with red 1-green 1.

Obviously there are also eleven ways for a 2 to show on the dice, but if you want to combine the chances of either a 1 or a 2 showing, the computation is not 11 + 11, but rather 11 + 9, since you must deduct two rolls, 2-1 and 1-2, which were already figured in determining the chances of a 1. Similarly, to allow for a 1, 2, or 3, the computation would be 11 + 9 + 7 (deducting four rolls, 3-1, 1-3, 3-2, and 2-3, already counted). Following through with all six numbers gives you 11 + 9 + 7 + 5 + 3 + 1 = 36, the same total reached by the simple 6 times 6 route.

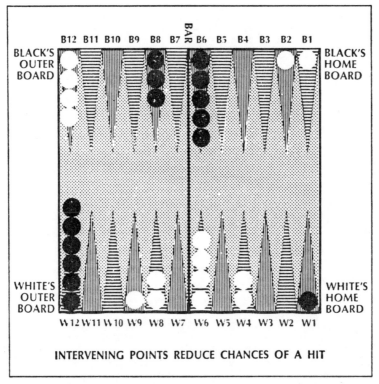

FIGURE 21

INTERVENING POINTS REDUCE CHANCES OF A HIT

Now let us return to the third facet in the expert's reasoning.

(3) The blot on W9 is a builder who can assist in making a useful blocked point in white's outer or home board. Running home with one's back men is only half the objective of the early game. The other is to block the opponent's back men from running. The devastating effect of a prime has already been demonstrated, but primes do not just happen. They are built and builders are needed to construct them. The blot left on W9 after the proper 4-1 opening move (Figure 20), is such a builder. His presence opens up eighteen additional ways—half the possible rolls—to make a useful point toward a prime:

- The bar point (W7) can be made with rolls of 6-2 (B12-W7, W9-W7) or 2-1 (W9-W7, W8-W7).

CHANCES OF HITTING A BLOT

To hit a blot this distance away	There are this number of direct shots	And this number of combination shots	So the total chances of a hit are
1	11	0	11
2	11	1	12
3	11	3	14
4	11	4	15
5	11	4	15
6	11	6	17
7	0	6	6
8	0	6	6
9	0	5	5
10	0	3	3
11	0	2	2
12	0	3	3
15	0	1	1
16	0	1	1
18	0	1	1
20	0	1	1
24	0	1	1
TOTALS	66	48	114*

* This strange total is verifiable thus: each role of two different numbers has three values—the number on one die, the number on the other, and the total of both dice. For example, on a 4-3 roll, one man can be advanced 3, 4, or 7 points. Three values for each of thirty permutations equals 90 values. Each of the six doubles has four values in backgammon—the number on the dice taken once, twice, three times, and four times—since a double counts as if four dice were cast and the same number turned up on all four. Six doubles times 4 values equals 24. Add 24 to the 90 values for dissimilar rolls and the total is 114 possibilities.

- W5 can be made with rolls of 4-3 (W9-W5, W8-W5) or 4-1 (W9-W5, W6-W5).
- W4: rolls of 5-4 (W9-W4, W8-W4) or 5-2 (W9-W4, W6-W4).
- W3: 6-5 (W9-W3, W8-W3) or 6-3 (W9-W3, W6-W3).
- W9 with any roll that includes a 4 (B12-W9). However, 6-4 is the only roll that truly applies, since the others are better used to make closer points.

We define a useful point as any one from the 3 point up through the 10 point. These are the only ones that can make a prime around W8 and W6, where the original setup of the board automatically gives you blocked points. You may wonder why a prime cannot be constructed from W6 through W11. The answer is that this would require a perfect dispersion of your men—one that is virtually impossible to achieve. There are already five men on W6, and they, of course, cannot be moved backward. That leaves ten men to be placed two each on the remaining five points of your desired prime. Every man has to be utilized just so, and there is no leeway. Your back men have to be brought forward quickly and efficiently and you cannot afford to have even one man hit.

A more realistic plan is to advance your third man from W8 and your third, fourth, and fifth men from W6 to help in building a prime. These men should be considered builders too, for they are not needed to maintain the point on their original location. Mid men also serve as builders, but they become more effective when they are brought into the outer board, for then one 5 or 6 roll can bring them into the home board.

Every game does not produce a prime. In fact, experienced players will hit blot after blot to prevent a prime. But each new blocked point you can build helps impede the opponent's back men, bringing you one step closer to victory. So, with a 4-1 opening roll, it is worthwhile to leave a blot on the 9 point. Sure, he can be hit by six possible rolls of your opponent. But you have eighteen ways to build a blocked point with him if he escapes an immediate hit. The odds are long in your favor.

Let's assume white moves first and takes his 4-1 roll as recommended. Further, black fails to hit the blot on the 9 point. That leaves white 32 chances out of 36 to make a useful point on his second roll—fourteen favorable opening rolls (see next chapter) plus the eighteen created by the builder on the 9 point.

(2) Splitting the back men doubles their chances of a hit. With the other half of the 4-1 roll white splits his back men (B1-B2). Say black now rolls a 5-4 and chooses to bring one mid man safely to B8 and to leave a blot at B9 with another mid man. That leaves the position in Figure 22. White's back man left on B1 can hit the blot in six ways—6-2, 5-3, double 4s and 2s. The

FIGURE 22

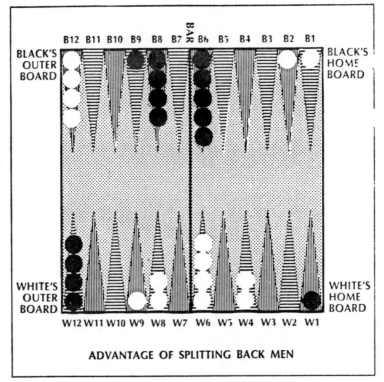

ADVANTAGE OF SPLITTING BACK MEN

back man you moved to B2 has six additional chances of a hit—
6-1 (moving the 1 first), 5-2 and 4-3.*So by splitting the back men
you double your chances for a hit. Sometimes you can do even
better: if black moves a mid man to B11, your chances for a hit
are increased from two to six by splitting; a blot on B10 is vulnerable to nine hits, compared to five if you hadn't split; and if
black is foolish enough to leave a blot on his bar point (B7), you
can hit him with twenty-eight rolls after a split (but a still respectable seventeen chances without the split).

The split enhances your running game as well. Double 5s,
ordinarily an awkward roll in the early game, can be used to
advance the back man from B2 safely to B12, or even further to
W8. Without the split, neither back man could move, as the first
5 lands on B6, where black has a point.

Unfortunately, 6-4 does not produce the same effect, as there
is no place to touch down with a 4 or a 6 from the 2 point. But
you can play 5-4 and 6-3 one point closer to your mid men than
otherwise, so it is a trifle less risky.

Splitting increases your chances of making a higher point in
your opponent's home board: 4-3 enables you to point on his 5
point, the most valuable one in backgammon (more on that in
the next chapter). 6-5 makes his bar point. 3-2 permits a point on
B4, 2-1 on B3. Even an otherwise useless 1 count brings your two
back men together again 1 point closer to home. Unless you
split your back men, only the four smallest doubles will make
a point within your opponent's home board. And doubles are
half as likely as dissimilar rolls.

(1) Your opponent probably will not hit your blots at B2 or
B1. Perhaps best of all, your two blots in black's home board are
quite safe. An experienced player seeks to make his points in
his home board as close as possible to the blocked points he al-

* By now it is hoped that you are accustomed to the concept that in the long
run each roll of two different numbers—each nondouble roll—occurs twice
in thirty-six throws. Therefore to save space and simplify the text such rolls
will be shown once, e.g., 6-2, rather than in both sequences, 6-2 and 2-6.

ready has. First preference is to make the 5 point, but the 4 and 3 points are also desirable. But the 2 and 1 points offer no real advantage until some of the others have been made, for there is no way to use them in a prime extending down from the blocked point that already exists on the 8 point. Pointing on the 2 or 1 point merely dissipates one's building strength and leaves gaps in the home board.

For all these reasons black won't hit your back men—unless he can hit both blots with a 4-1 roll, which is otherwise a neutral roll. Hitting two blots with one roll is generally winning tactics unless this leaves two blots in one's home board. The *double bump* (or hit) wastes the opponent's next roll. Both halves must be played to bring the men off the bar, and if the number on one die matches a blocked point, then the opponent is hamstrung for an additional roll.

The blots on B1 and B2 can also be double hit with a 6-5 roll, but in actual play they won't because there is a far better move available, as we shall soon see in the next chapter.

CHAPTER III
The Early Moves

You have two objectives in the early game: (1) run with your back men before they are hemmed in, and (2) try to build blocked points on your side of the board to prevent your opponent's back men from escaping. In your first roll or two you need not choose between these two goals; the dice will make the decision for you.

The best rolls of all are those that make your 5 or bar points (W5 or W7), for they start you on the way to a prime. The bar point may seem preferable, since it gives you three consecutive points, but in fact, the 5 point is universally recognized as the most desirable for several sound reasons.

- It deprives your opponent of one landing point for his man on the bar.
- It forces a man on the bar to come out on a lower number, so you may still be able to hem him in or bump him.
- It aids in the progressive development of your home board, thereby enhancing the value of points on W4 or W3. The first would give you three consecutive points toward a prime; the second leaves a gap of one point (W4), which you hope to fill later.

- It starts to limit the mobility of black's back men. For example, a back man cannot be played to a 5-4 roll.
- It deprives black of his best defensive outpost. If *he* makes your 5 point, he has a direct shot at all your men coming into your outer board. Moreover, his men on W5 can begin their run home with comparative ease when their time comes. A blockade from W11 down to hold them in check is virtually impossible. In contrast, when black's back men are left at W1, they can easily be blocked, unless black keeps harassing you elsewhere.
- It is an additional safe refuge for your men as they come homeward.

FIGURE 23

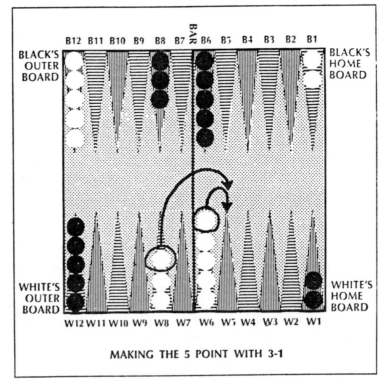

MAKING THE 5 POINT WITH 3-1

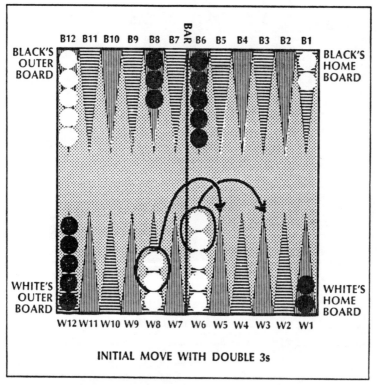

FIGURE 24

INITIAL MOVE WITH DOUBLE 3s

POINT-MAKING MOVES

Three opening rolls enable you to make your 5 point: 3-1, double 3s and double 1s.* The correct moves are shown in Figures 23, 24, and 25. The two double rolls are particularly useful, since they make *two* points in your home board.

Double 4s can also be played to make the 5 point: take two men from B12 all the way to W5, touching down first on W9. However, most experts prefer to make the opponent's 5 point and bring in two mid men only as far as W9 (Figure 26).

Only two other rolls—6-1 and double 6s—will make the bar

---

* A double cannot be the initial roll, since the dice must be recast to determine who moves first. But generally the second player moves his doubles the same way, regardless of the first move. For that reason, doubles are discussed here.

FIGURE 25

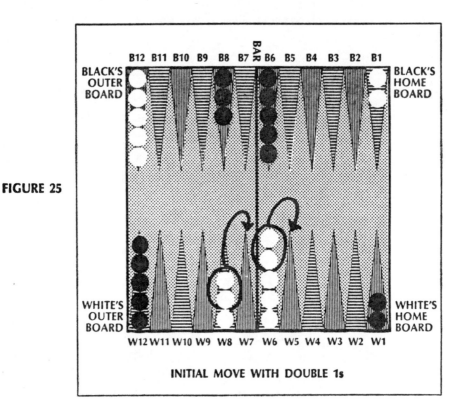

INITIAL MOVE WITH DOUBLE 1s

FIGURE 26

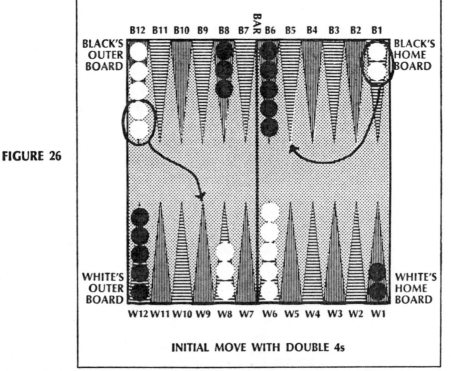

INITIAL MOVE WITH DOUBLE 4s

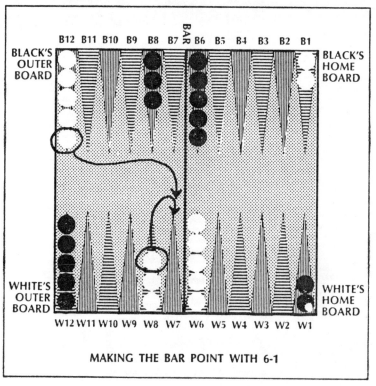

FIGURE 27

MAKING THE BAR POINT WITH 6-1

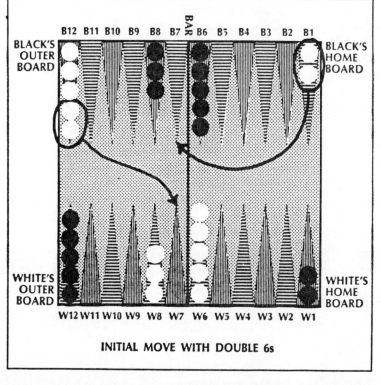

FIGURE 28

INITIAL MOVE WITH DOUBLE 6s

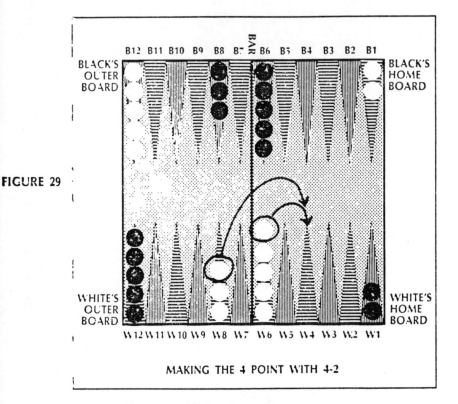

FIGURE 29

MAKING THE 4 POINT WITH 4-2

point (Figures 27 and 28). Both are strong rolls, but double 6s is the stronger: it gives you control of both bar points and allows you to play either a running or a blocking game.

The 4 point is next in preference, for it helps to block the opponent's back men while leaving only a one-point gap as you build downward from W6 in your inner board. Either a roll of 4-2 or double 2s conventionally makes the 4 point (Figures 29 and 30).

Going one step further, the 3 point can be made with a 5-3 roll (Figure 31). Many experts, however, see little real benefit in making the 3 point so early in the game, so they play this roll as a building move, which will be explained shortly. The 3 point becomes more desirable once the 5 point has been made, for

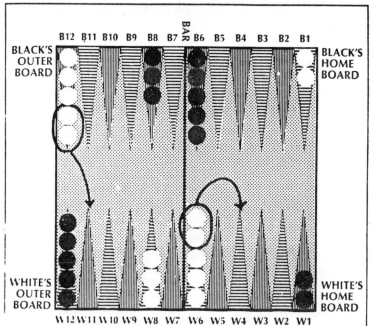

FIGURE 30

INITIAL MOVE WITH DOUBLE 2s

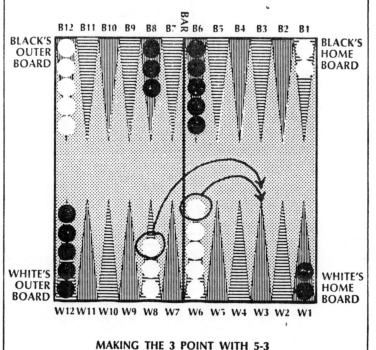

FIGURE 31

MAKING THE 3 POINT WITH 5-3

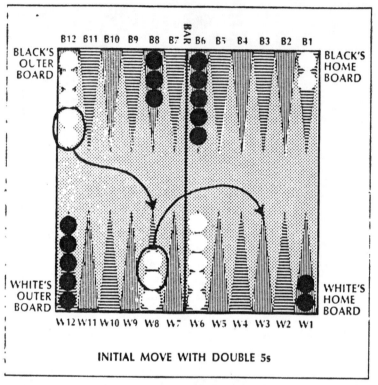

FIGURE 32

INITIAL MOVE WITH DOUBLE 5s

there is but one open point inbetween. Later, if W7 or W4 are made, only one more point is needed to make a prime.

Double 5s also make the 3 point: move two men from B12 all the way to W3, touching down on W8 (Figure 32). Unfortunately, this move is an embarrassment of riches, as it thrusts two mid men all the way to make a dubious point in your home board, leaving but three mid men to help make the more desirable points. Nonetheless, this is the least damaging way to play double 5s. Ordinarily, a double is a beneficial roll in the early game, but this is the exception.

It may seem like splitting hairs to write off the 3 point as "dubious" while advocating the 5, bar, and 4 points as "desirable." But there is logic behind this distinction. Remember you start with blocked points on W8 and W6. These are the cornerstones on which you hope to build a prime—or at least four or five adjoining points. Given free rein, you would make your 5 point, then the bar point to give you a series of four points with no gaps. Then you would work forward, first making W4 and then W3 (or W8) to complete a prime.

As every backgammon buff ruefully acknowledges, the dice are fickle. So, count your blessings when you can make your 4 point. That leaves only a one-point gap—the revered 5 point—but you still have plenty of mid men and outer men to help make that point later, opposed only by the two seemingly helpless black back men.

By comparison, making the 3 point is no cause for rejoicing, for it leaves a gap of two points from W6. Black's back men on W1 have an almost equal chance of occupying one of those two inviting spots, or of running to safety before you occupy them.

In short, you try to build gradually downward from your 8 and 6 points, leaving a one-point gap when you must. But a two-point gap is questionable, not that we admit any animus to the 3 point. On the contrary, once we have made the 5 or 4 point, we covet it.

All of the foregoing rolls we call *point-makers*, for that is exactly what they accomplish. These are the most desirable opening rolls—with the exception of double 5s—for the reasons just stated. Not only do these moves hem in black's back men and start the process of building a prime, but they also provide safe landing places for your men as they come around; each new man that comes to rest on a point you have made is a builder who can help to make a new point.

RUNNING MOVES

Other rolls are best suited to running the back men into black's outer board, hoping they do not get hit. Only one roll,

6-5, affectionally named the *lover's leap*, brings a back man to complete safety on B12 (Figure 33).

A 6-4 roll is played the same way (Figure 34), but lands one point short of safety. The resultant blot on B11 can be hit if

FIGURE 33

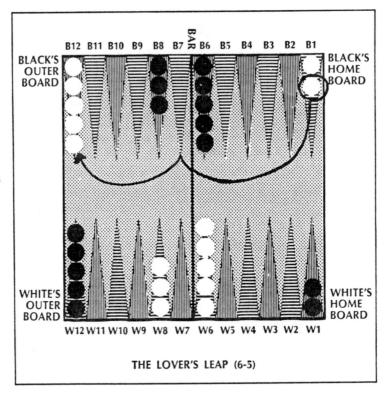

THE LOVER'S LEAP (6-5)

black now rolls one of the eleven combinations that include a 2. (In the table of probabilities there are twelve rolls that hit a blot two points away, but in this case double 1s are useless, since black cannot touch down on the intervening point blocked by white. This is still another illustration of why you should figure the odds with each situation as it arises.)

We will hold the 6-3 and 6-2 rolls for later, since in expert circles they are not played as a full running move. The expert reasons that if he runs a back man out to B10 on a 6-3 roll, his opponent has thirteen ways to hit the blot. Whereas if a back man runs to B9 on a 6-2 roll, the opponent has fourteen ways to hit him. Experts are very stingy about leaving unnecessary blots in their opponent's outer board. A combination shot is needed to hit

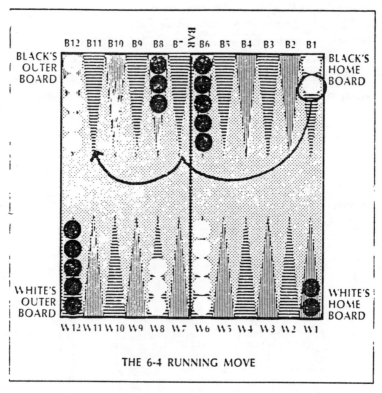

FIGURE 34

THE 6-4 RUNNING MOVE

right back in the same spot and the odds are better than 6 to 1 against a return hit. The expert who plays thousands of games in his lifetime begrudges his opponent the extra shots that are afforded by running with 6-3 and 6-2. For a beginner, though, no disaster will strike if he chooses to run one back man out with these two rolls.

BUILDING MOVES

If the opening roll is not a point-maker, and is not suitable for running a back man, then it is best used to bring a builder into your outer board where he can help to make a useful point later.

A 4-3 roll, for example, is best played by bringing in two builders from B12 to W9 and W10 (Figure 35). This may seem an innocuous move, or perhaps even a foolhardy one, since black's men on W1 can hit one of your blots with any roll totaling 8 or 9. Still, that is only eleven chances out of thirty-six, and observe what happens if he fails to hit your blot; no matter what you

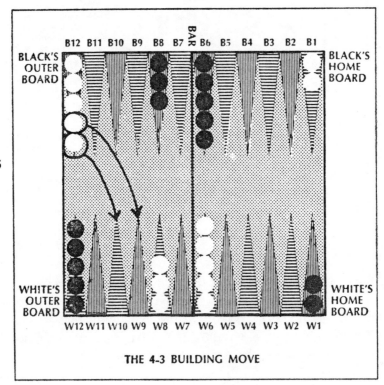

THE 4-3 BUILDING MOVE

roll the next time, you will be able to make a useful point—on W5, W7, W4, or W3. Try it out on your own board. Of course, the original setup of the boards permits you to make a useful point with fourteen rolls, but the flexibility of the builders on W9 and W10 now allow you to use the other twenty-two rolls as point-makers. You may have to leave a blot after your second roll, but that is a small price to pay for getting a useful point early.

A 3-2 roll also brings in two builders, to W10 and W11 (Figure 36). This is almost as good as the 4-3 move. Only one roll—5-4—fails to cover a blot, while a 5-2 roll can only be used to cover the blot on W12, not a really useful point. Still, that leaves 32 point-makers out of 36, or an 89% chance.

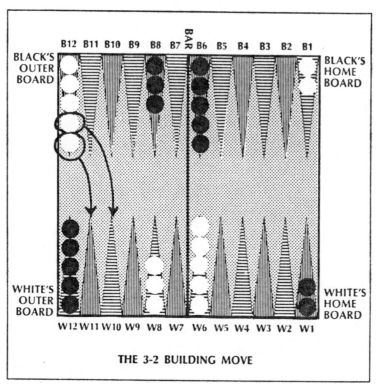

FIGURE 36

THE 3-2 BUILDING MOVE

Each of the remaining two building moves—5-2 and 5-4—bring in only one useful builder (Figures 37 and 38). The 5 must be used to bring a mid man to W8, which already has a surplus man as a builder. These two rolls are not considerd favorable, but there is a correct way to play each. Earlier, we pointed out that some experts use the 5-3 roll as a building move, rather than as a point-maker. This alternative is shown in Figure 39.

FIGURE 37

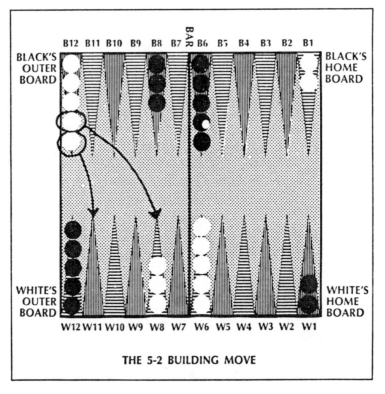

THE 5-2 BUILDING MOVE

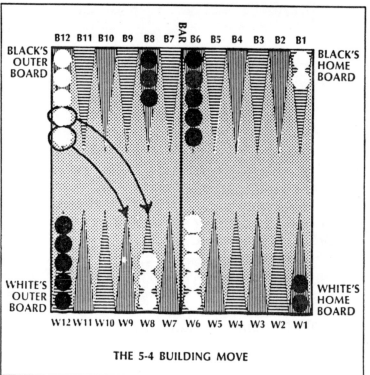

THE 5-4 BUILDING MOVE

FIGURE 38

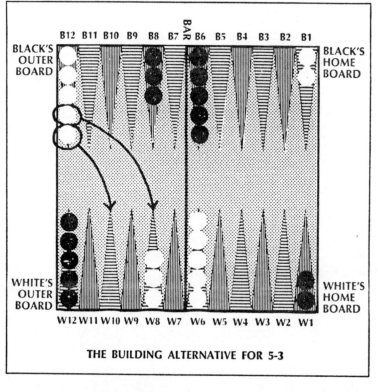

THE BUILDING ALTERNATIVE FOR 5-3

FIGURE 39

SPLIT-AND-BUILD MOVES

A count of 1 on a die cannot be used as a builder, for the black men on W12 block you from moving your mid men there. Unless the roll is a 6-1 or 3-1 point-maker, the preferred move is to split the back men, moving one to B2, and use the other half of the roll to send in a builder. Thus with a 4-1 or 2-1 roll, the larger die brings in a builder to W9 or W11 (Figures 40 and 41).

Although splitting your back men leaves them quite safe from attack, there are several double rolls with which black could point on one of your blots. Only one should concern you: double 5s. Ordinarily an awkward roll to play, it now allows black to hit your blot on B1 with two home men and to bring in two outer men to make a point at B3 (Figure 42). Establishing the 1 point this early weakens black's game, but as compensation he has also made an intermediate point at B3. The effort has depleted his forces, so he will try to bring some mid men quickly as builders to make points on B5, B4 and B2, which would give him a strong position.

The other double rolls that allow black to point on your blot are not so threatening:

- Double 4s: black could play this the same way as double 5s—hitting your blot—this time on B2—with two home men and sending in two outer men to make an intermediate point—this time on B4. This looks even better than the double 5s play, for each of black's new point is one step closer to the anchor at B6. The difference is that double 4s is an excellent roll, permitting black to make useful points at W5 and B9. If he elects to hitting instead, you haven't really lost anything.
- Double 2s: to point on the blot at B1 uses up black's entire roll and does not make an intermediate point. The superior play is to move mid men and two home men to make points at B11 and B4.

There is danger from another quarter in splitting your back men: the double bump. With a 4-1 roll black moves a home man four points to hit your blot on B2, then one point to hit the man

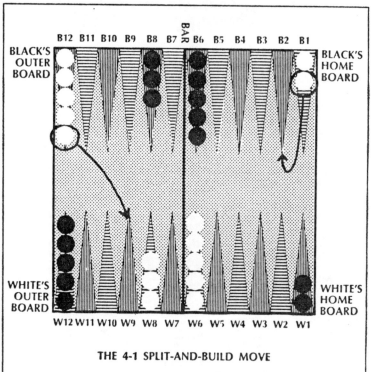

FIGURE 40

THE 4-1 SPLIT-AND-BUILD MOVE

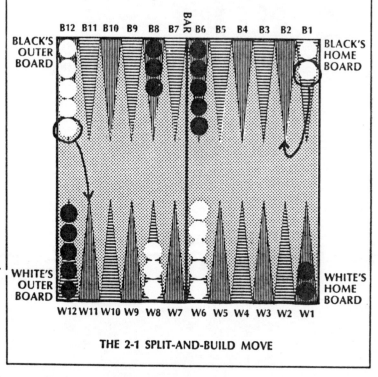

FIGURE 41

THE 2-1 SPLIT-AND-BUILD MOVE

on B1 (Figure 43). The double bump is a productive tactic, unless it creates two blots in one's home board. Therefore, black should not use a 6-5 or a 6-1 roll to hit twice for this would leave two blots open to any of twenty hitting rolls on white's next turn. Instead he should make his normal move.

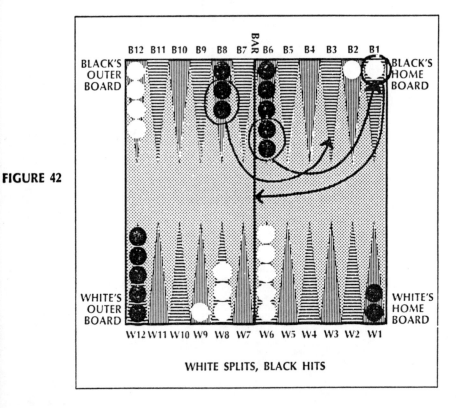

FIGURE 42

WHITE SPLITS, BLACK HITS

Now let's return to the last of the splitting rolls: 5-1. One back man splits to B2 and a mid man advances to W8 (Figure 44). Not very constructive, as you already have a point there. In fact, it is one of the worst opening rolls to play, unless you are a staunch believer in safety first. We have experimented with running a back man out to B7 on an early 5-1 roll. If black hits the

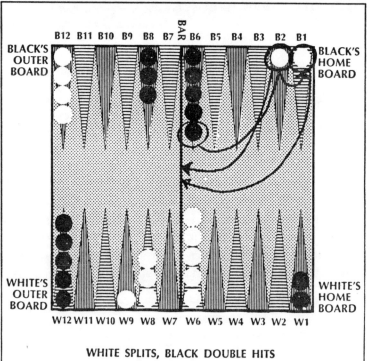

FIGURE 43

WHITE SPLITS, BLACK DOUBLE HITS

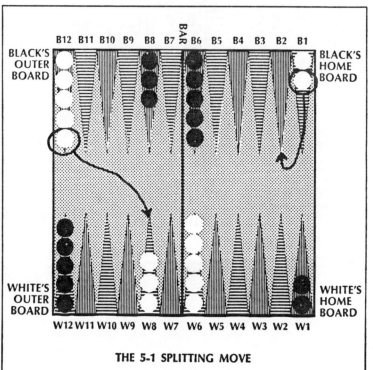

FIGURE 44

THE 5-1 SPLITTING MOVE

blot but cannot cover, you have fourteen ways to bump him right back—any 6 roll except double 6s, plus 5-2 and 4-3, which permit the man on the bar to come in and hit. However, if black fails to hit your blot, you have seventeen ways to make his bar point, which would give you a vantage point from which to hit his men as they come around to his outer board.

RUN-AND-BUILD MOVES

A 6 roll creates an awkward situation when it does not fit into the point-making (6-1) or running (6-5, 6-4) categories. The expert plays the remaining roles—6-3 and 6-2—as *run-and-build* moves. He runs a back man out to B7 with the 6 and sends a build-

FIGURE 45

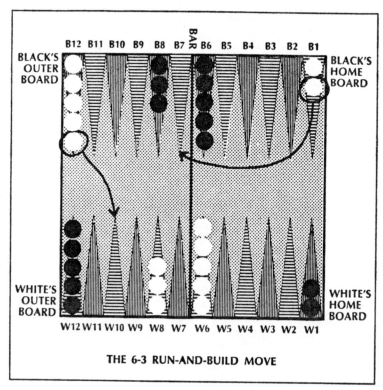

THE 6-3 RUN-AND-BUILD MOVE

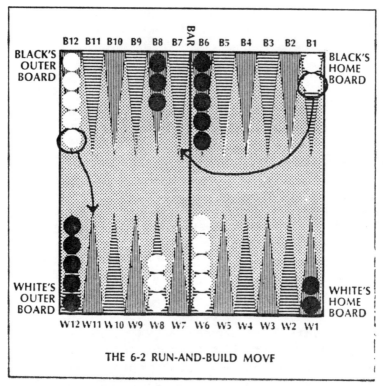

FIGURE 46

THE 6-2 RUN-AND-BUILD MOVE

er from B12 with the other die (Figures 45 and 46).

To recap, the best moves are the point-makers, next the running moves, and lastly the building moves. With an awkward combination, you run with the 6 and send in a builder with the other number.

SHORTCUT SUMMARY OF OPENING MOVES

Here is a synopsis to aid in remembering the recommended moves on the opening roll. The rolls they apply to are given in parentheses:

1. *Two different numbers on the dice*
   - Special rule for 6s:

a. Run with the two highest (6-5, 6-4).
b. Run-and-build with the next two (6-3, 6-2).
c. Make your bar point with the smallest (6-1).

- All other numbers
  a. If the difference in the dice is 2, make a point in your inner board (5-3, 4-2, 3-1).
  b. Otherwise, bring in two builders if you can (5-4, 5-2, 4-3, 3-2)
  c. When you can't—because a 1 turns up (5-1, 4-1, 2-1 —split a back man with the 1.

2. *Doubles* (for the player who rolls second)
   - Even numbers (6s, 4s, 2s): move exactly two mid men. With 6s and 4s also move two back men. With 2s move two *home* men ("smallest number is closest to *home*").
   - Odd numbers: make two new points in your home board if you can (3s, 5s if there is a blot on W1).
   - Otherwise make points in this priority: W5 (1s), W7 (1s), W3 (3s, 5s when there is no blot on W1).
   - Don't leave a blot. This applies particularly to double 5s. After you move two outer men to W3, cover the blot at W8 with two mid men. Stated differently, you should move two mid men all the way.

FRIVOLOUS BLOTS

None of the recommended moves leave a frivolous blot within either home board. A blot on B2 is not frivolous, as we have painstakingly shown. A blot on B3, B4, or B5 on the other hand is decidedly frivolous, as we shall now show.

Advancing a back man past B2 puts black's outer man in range to score a double hit with rolls of 4-3 or 5-2. With a 4-3 roll, black plays the 3 first to hit a blot on B5 and his 4 first to hit on B4. In either case he completes his roll with a hit at B1. A 5-2 roll double-hits at B3 and B1. Both rolls are otherwise innocuous, so black will be silently thankful for your giving him a constructive way to play them.

Worse is yet to come. What if black rolls one of the fourteen point-making rolls, and the point happens to be where you left your blot? This makes black's move doubly sweet—to him.

And what could you possibly gain by the extra step or two past B2? Inching up for a later running move? It just is not worth the risks.

Leaving a blot in your home board is even more dangerous. Not that you cannot afford to have that man sent to the bar, for you have plenty of troops available for building. But you lose a tempo in preparing your board. Unless you next roll a double, half your next play is wasted so you cannot make a combination point-making move. Furthermore, black may be able to cover the man that hit your blot or else run him toward home.

Dropping a blot on the 5 point is something else again. The 5 point is so valuable that some fine players go all out to make it. On a 5-3 roll, for example, they may bring a man from B12 to W5. (We have seen the same play with a 6-2 roll, but less frequently.) Or, on a 5-1 roll, they drop a man from W6 to W5 and send a mid man to W8. The effect of all three moves is to leave a blot at W5. Black can hit the blot with any of fifteen rolls. But if he does not, white can cover with any of twenty-four rolls—any 1, 3, or 8. It sound like long odds for white, but actually he is about a 3% underdog, since black rolls first.

A 2-1 roll gives a slight variation. White drops a home man to W5, but brings in a mid man as a builder to W11. Black can hit one of the blots in seventeen ways (a 6-4 hits at W11), but white has thirty-one ways to cover if black misses (including 6-5, 6-4, 4-2, and double 6s, all of which bring the man on W11 to W5). We prefer this move, but it still leaves black with about a 2% edge, because he rolls next.

It may seem foolish to make a move that has less than an even chance for success, but you do not mind having your blot hit early in the game, while the advantage of scoring your 5 point is considerable. So you willingly take the chance.

Besides, the risk is less than it seems. Seven of the rolls that hit your blot on W5 are excellent point-makers for black—double 4s, 2s, 1s, and 4-2, 3-1. Black would make a forward-going move with any of these rolls anyway, so you really have not lost much if he elects to hit your blot instead.

This brings up a very important backgammon principle: try to create positions where your opponent has the fewest possible "good rolls" and the greatest number of "bad rolls." Avoid placing your men so that his awkward rolls suddenly become advantageous. Conversely, move your men so that your chances of rolling an embarrassing number are reduced to a minimum.

Of course, this requires great foresight, quick calculation, and considerable experience, particularly since the opponent's moves exert pressure and reduce your options. A beginner cannot hope to analyze in this fashion. Keep the principle in mind, though, for it will improve your game immeasurably in the long run.

Observe, too, how few disastrous rolls befall the top players in the end game. The casual kibitzer chalks this up to luck, but the true explanation is the expert player has developed a position where few rolls can be disastrous.

You can prove this by jotting down a complicated late position in an expert game and then working out at leisure how you would handle each of the possible rolls. If, say, two-thirds of them enhance the expert's chances, you are witnessing top backgammon—not sheer luck.

Before going further, the reader is urged to review the opening moves once again on the following two lists and to play out each move on the board in back.

OPENING MOVES—BY CATEGORY

1. Point-makers
   5-3 makes point at W3 (W8-W3, W6-W3)
   4-2 makes point at W4 (W8-W4, W6-W4)
   3-1 makes point at W5 (W8-W5, W6-W5
   6-1 makes bar point (B12-W7, W8-W7)
   Double 6s makes both bar points (2 men from B1-B7, 2 men from B12-W7)
   Double 5s makes point at W3 (2 men from B12-W3)
   Double 4s makes points at W9 and B5 (2 men from B12-W9, 2 men from B1-B5)
   Double 3s makes points at W5 and W3 (2 men from W8-W5, 2 men from W6-W3)
   Double 2s makes points at W11 and W4 (2 men from B12-W11, 2 men from W6-W4)
   Double 1s makes bar and 5 points (2 men from W8-W7, 2 men from W6-W5)

2. Running moves
   6-5 (B1-B12)
   6-4 (B1-B11)

3. Building moves
   5-4 (B12-W8, B12-W9)
   5-2 (B12-W8, B12-W11)
   4-3 (B12-W9, B12-W10)
   3-2 (B12-W10, B12, W11)

4. Splitting moves (split-and-build)
   5-1 (B12-W8, B1-B2)
   4-1 (B12-W9, B1-B2)
   2-1 (B12-W11, B1-B2)

5. Run-and-build moves
   6-3 (B1-B7, B12-W10)
   6-2 (B1-B7, B12-W11)

OPENING MOVES—IN NUMERICAL SEQUENCE

6-6: 2 from B1-B7, 2 from B12-W7
6-5: B1-B12
6-4: B1-B11
6-3: B1-B7, B12-W10
6-2: B1-B7, B12-W11
6-1: B12-W7, W8-W7
5-5: 2 from B12 to W3
5-4: B12-W8, B12-W9
5-3: W8-W3, W6-W3
5-2: B12-W8, B12-W11
5-1: B12-W8, B1-B2
4-4: 2 from B1-B5, 2 from B12-W9
4-3: B12-W9, B12-W10
4-2: W8-W4, W6-W4
4-1: B12-W9, B1-B2
3-3: 2 from W8-W5, 2 from W6-W3
3-2: B12-W10, B12-W11
3-1: W8-W5, W6-W5
2-2: 2 from B12-W11, 2 from W6-W4
2-1: B12-W11, B1-B2
1-1: 2 from W8-W7, 2 from W6-W5

THE REPLY TO THE OPENING MOVE

When your opponent wins the opening roll, you should usually play your roll exactly as if you went first. But some adjustments should be made for the new deployment of the opposing men. Here are a few guidelines to your action:

- Hit a blot when you can. It will cost your opponent at least half his next roll just to bring the man off the bar. Thus, he can't use both dice to make a point on his side of the table.
- Hit two blots with gusto when the opportunity is presented— unless this creates two blots in your home board.

- Do not leave a man vulnerable to two direct shots. Black will hit joyfully for the reasons just given.
- When black has made a point in his home board, think seriously about running one of your back men with any roll totally 8 or more. Do not take half measures, though—use the entire roll to run. Stopping at B7 gives black two direct shots at you. Since he has made a second point in his home board, and you have not, he will be happy to exchange pot shots with you. His man's odds of coming off the bar are 35 to 1. Yours are only 8 to 1.* Moreover, the times he hits on B7 and you cannot hit right back spell real trouble for you. Black is an odds-on favorite to cover at B7, giving him four consecutive points toward a prime, leaving you a decided underdog.
- Do not panic because black has made his 5 point. Make a useful point of your own and you will be just about even. Otherwise, on a large roll run a back man to black's outer board. Use a small roll to inch forward in black's home board, hoping to get out on the next roll. But you must take some concrete action, for black is starting to close in on your back men. Unless you exert equal pressure or prepare to get out, your mobility will be further curtailed as he makes additional *interior points.*

TO HIT OR TO POINT

From time to time you will be faced with the delightful dilemma of hitting versus making a good point. Should you turn from temptation and go about your business of building your board?

No. A man on the bar throws its owner off stride. You have stolen half his next roll. When it turns out to be a choice pointmaker, like 3-1, he cannot enjoy its benefit. And 6-1 is even more frustrating. Black must come out on the 1, as your 6 point is blocked. What can he then do with the 6? A blot on either bar

* Double 6s is the only roll that keeps him on the bar. Double 6s, 5s, and 6-5 keep you there.

point invites trouble, but the alternative of shooting an outer man to B2 is even worse. By one simple hit you convert a desirable roll into a horror.

We will even hit with 3-1 when black has run a man out to W9 or W10. We will feel sheepish when he counters with a large roll that bumps us in the same spot, but it is some solace to know we played with the odds.

However, we will not waste three-quarters of a double to make a hit. Better to make two interior points—or one inside and one outside.

There are positive virtues to a judicious hit. When you hit a blot in your outer board, you also deploy a builder there. When the hit is in black's outer board, you also bring a back man part way home. Black has only half a roll with which to hit back. Say you hit at B10. Ordinarily, black has thirteen direct shots at the blot you leave. Now he has but nine: one number of a 2-1 roll is needed to bring the man off the bar; and he must come out on the 3 of a 6-3.

Parents admonish their children not to point or hit. In backgammon, both actions are admirable. At the highest level, the verdict is: hit, rather than point. For backgammon has two faces: setting an opponent back counts as much, or more, toward victory as bringing your own men forward. With that distinction in mind, decide your action in the quiz that follows. Set up the board in back in the starting position. Then make black's opening move, as given. After each question reset the pieces to the opening position.

QUIZ 3
REPLY TO THE OPENING MOVE

1. Set up each problem on the PRACTI-GAMMON® board in the back of the book. Black makes his 4 point with a 4-2 roll (B8-B4, B6-B4). How would you play:

   a. 6-3?

   b. 6-2?

2. Black played his 5-2 roll as a builder, moving two mid men to B11 and B8. How do you move a 6-3 roll?

3. On a 6-3 black ran a back man to W10 (in disregard of our recommendation). Play a 5-3 roll in reply.

4. Black again makes an unorthodox play. With 6-2 he moves two mid men, to B11 and B7. What do you do with:

   a. 6-4?

   b. 6-3?

   c. 6-2?

   d. 6-1?

5. Black makes his 5 point on a 3-1 (B8-B5, B6-B5). How do you counter with a 5-3 roll?

6. Black runs a back man to W11 on a 6-4 roll. What is your reply with:

   a. 6-4?

   b. 6-3?

7. Black splits his back men on 4-1 (W1-W2, W12-B9). How do you reply with:

   a. another 4-1?

   b. double 5s?

ANSWERS TO QUIZ 3
REPLY TO THE OPENING MOVE

1. a. and b. Run a back man all the way with both rolls, to B10 and B9, respectively. Ordinarily, you would stop at B7 and bring a builder in with the smaller number. However, when black makes an interior point, you should not tarry on his bar point—too easy and tempting a hit.

2. Run-and-build (B1-B7, B12-W10). Even if you customarily run with 6-3, this is not the time for this move. You would land just in front of black's man at B11, handing black two direct shots—a 1 from B11 and a 3 from W12—or twenty hitting rolls. The blot you leave on B7 is

open to direct shots from three points, W12, B11, and B8,—twenty-nine possible rolls—but with this difference: you will have a direct shot in return from B1.

3. Hit the blot with your 3 (B12-W10) and use the 5 to bring in another mid man (B12-W8). Do not use the entire roll for one man to drop a blot on W5, since both the man on the bar and the one on W1 will have shots at him (twenty-one rolls, too many to justify dropping a blot in your own home board).

4. a. Make your regular running move to B11, double-hitting on the way (be sure to move your 6 first!).
   b. Hit the blot on B7 and send in a mid man as a builder to W10.
   c. Hit the blot on B7 and bring in a builder to W11.
   d. Make your bar point (W8-W7, B12-W7). You would hit the blot if you could only find a decent move for the 1: (W6-W5) is too risky (see comment for problem 3); (B1-B2) looks harmless, but that destroys your only playable 6 should you next roll a 6 (either B12-W7 or W8-W2 hurts your game).

   Note that in all four situations you end up with the standard move, but for different reasons. You hit a blot unless you have an outstanding point-making move that becomes unplayable as a hit move. Also observe how black's blot on his bar point improves your rolls in a, b, and c. You would also have hit with 5-1, 4-2, double 3s (sending both back man to B7), but not with double 2s (better to make points at W4 and W11).

5. Run a back man (moving the 3 first) to B9, better than making a dubious point at W3. Black's pointing on B5 is your signal to run, unless you can make an equally valuable point.

6. Play both rolls as a run-and-build move (B1-B7, B12-W9 and-W10 respectively). Running all the way would give black two direct shots—from W11 and W12.

7. a. Hit both blots in your home board (W6-W2-W1). This destroys black's next roll and is worth the risk of a return hit (only eleven chances, at that).
   b. Point on the blot at B1 (two men from W6-W1) and make your 3 point (two men from W8-W3), giving you three interior points. You plan to bring in your mid men to reestablish your point on W8 and make other valuable points on W7, W5, and W4.

SUMMARY

In the first few moves try to:

- Make points in your home board to block black's back men.
- Bring in builders to your outer board to help make additional points.
- Run with your back men to black's outer board.
- With few exceptions, hit any exposed blot.

CHAPTER IV

Winning Tactics and a Sample Game

The reader who has mastered the opening moves and the replies has every reason to feel he has come a long way. If he also understands the distinctions among point-making, building, and running moves and the various combinations, he is well on his way to becoming a worthy opponent.

There is still a long road to travel, for the balance of the game demands more than memory. No matter, for the principles underlying the opening moves persist throughout the game.

WHERE YOU HAVE THE EDGE

Examine the original setup of the pieces (Figure 2, page 18). Then ask yourself whether you have an advantage on either side of the table. At first glance, there seems little to choose from: on your side you have eight men situated on two points, while your opponent has seven, also on two points. A slight advantage on your side.

Actually, your edge is overpowering, since black's mid men do not figure in the contest on your side of the table. They cannot move backward into your outer or home boards. But your mid men just over the boundary line, move in the opposite direction and can be brought in easily to build points, make them immediately, or hit blots. Adding your five mid men and subtracting black's five mid men nets a 13 to 2 edge for you and three blocked points to black's one.

Such a one-sided advantage would make backgammon unplayable except that the situation is exactly duplicated in reverse on the opposite side of the table. You are strong on your side, just where black is weakest. He is overpowering on his side, where you are most vulnerable. So you start out on equal terms.

Still, the distinction between the two sides of the table is crucial to winning tactics. The running moves, for example, may seem absurd to a player who does not distinguish between white's and black's starting positions. "Why," he muses, "should I use a 6-4 roll to bring out a back man to your 11 point, where you have a direct shot at him? I shall wait until I roll 6-5 and can run him safely to my mid men."

He may wait a long time. A 6-5 roll comes up, on the average, twice in thirty-six rolls. When it does, it may be too late to run, for the opponent may have made his bar point by then. But let us assume good fortune: an early 6-5 roll and an open bar point. One back man escapes in safety to join his mid men. The other, though, is left alone and defenseless against thirteen enemies bearing down on him. Eventually one will make the hit, covered on the same roll, or perhaps later. By that time the opponent may have four, five, or even all six points in his home board secured. Frequently that one hit decides the game. For want of two early 6-5 rolls our foolish friend has chucked the game.

The more practical player senses his weakness on the opposite side of the table. He does not wait for the perfect 6-5 roll, but is content to run with 6-4—or 6-3 or 6-2. Certainly his man may be hit, but there are few sure things in backgammon.

All backgammon men are not equal—in the starting position. Consider your back men as courageous runners of a gauntlet in black's home board. Sometime or other, each will have to make his move. So when a suitable roll comes up, he must venture forth, before his enemies close his escape route. Even an early run subjects him to a direct shot, but later he would face many guns. If he cowardly stays back, he may never get out at all. But at least he has no fear of a hit there. For he has a companion and together they make an inviolate point.

Only when he steps out into black's outer board is he truly defenseless. Short of B12, there is no safe place to stop. And he has only long-range (combination) shots at whatever blots black may have left en route.

By contrast, he has fire power and support within black's home table. If he moves off B1 and is hit, he or his companion can hit right back. On the occasion that black hits and covers on the same roll, he may succeed in rejoining the other back man to reestablish a point. Yes, eventually he must start on the trip home, else he will be trapped and the game probably lost. But while he is in black's home board, he can defend himself.

Only in black's outer board is he heavily outgunned. That is black's free-fire zone and your most dangerous quarter of the playing field.

Now look at the brighter side. Your outer board is your safest haven in the early game. The builders you bring in there are open to combination shots only—the correct total of both dice—at worst, one chance in six. So bring them in early and fear not to leave blots.

Beginners are nervous about leaving blots anywhere and do not distinguish between dangerous and safe quadrants. Consequently, they rarely miss a chance to cover a blot. In their haste they frequently fail to see that they could have improved their position by making a more valuable point. An easy way to ensure against passing up these good moves is as follows:

GUIDELINE TO POINTING

Subtract the numerals of your two dice. See if the difference matches the distance between any two of your blots or builders.

White rolls a 6-4 in Figure 47. At first glance there seems to be a choice of rotten apples: run with the other back man, leaving two direct shots for black's mid men (twenty chances) or make your 2 point prematurely.

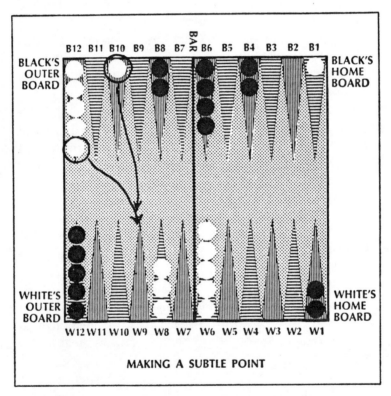

FIGURE 47

MAKING A SUBTLE POINT

Now apply the guideline. Subtracting 4 from 6 leaves 2. You have men at B12 and B10—also two points apart. On B12 you have a builder—a surplus man—and on B10, a blot. According to our guideline, they should make a point. Move the nearer man (B12) the smaller number (4) to W9 and the further man (B10) the larger number (6) also to W9. You have made a valuable point and have three points toward a prime.

Black rolls 3-1 and makes his 5 point. That is a classic point-making roll, but the guideline would work if black were not familiar with the opening moves: 3-1 = B8-B6.

Now you roll 4-1—a difference of 3—and look for blots or builders three points apart, W9 and W6. But wait: W9 has no blot or builder; both men are needed to secure the point. Still, W5 is more valuable than W9, so you give up one point to make another for a net gain in position. Moreover, you now have a true builder at W9 out of range of a direct shot from W1.

EXCEPTIONS

Alas, the guideline sometimes disappoints. In Figure 48 you roll 6-5. The difference is 1, as is the margin between your men on B11 and B12. True enough they will join up, but on W8, where you already have a point. So you do not follow the rule blindly, but make the classic running move instead (B1-B12).

A second exception occurs in Figure 49. On a 4-2 roll you can move a home man and an outer man to point on W4, but that creates a blot on W6 subject to a hit with any 5 roll (fifteen possibilities). A hit there would remove a vital point toward your prime, so you look around for another move. Decide before reading further.

The safe and sensible move is bringing in two more builders from B12—to W9 and W11. A more daring play is to move just one mid man to W7. Like the first move—pointing on W4—this exposes a blot, but no point is relinquished. More important, if black fails to hit your man (any 6 except double 2s, or sixteen chances), you have three stations from which to cover—B12, W9, W8—and twenty-eight ways to cover. It is less than an even-money gamble (the mathematics are too complicated to give here) but justified by the possible gain—five points toward a prime—versus the small loss—if your blot is sent to the bar he can join your one remaining back man. Generally, two men in black's home board give you a better position than one, since you may be able to put them together for a point.

The one real drawback to the move to W7 is that black has more points made in his home board than you have in yours. Thus, he has the advantage should a *blot-hitting contest* develop (each player hitting at every opportunity in a loose game with plenty of blots lying around). You will have twenty-seven ways to come off the bar, but he will have thirty-two. Offhand, you might be willing to look only at your own odds and conclude that twenty-seven chances, or 75%, is ample. But each time you exchange hits you would be bucking the odds. Look at it this way: if you

FIGURE 48

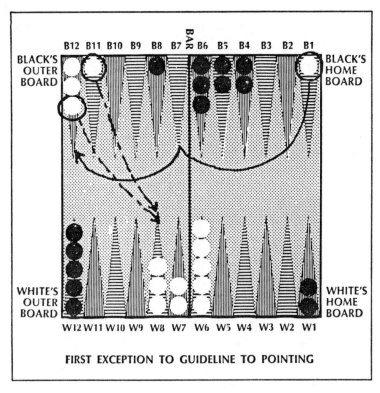

FIRST EXCEPTION TO GUIDELINE TO POINTING

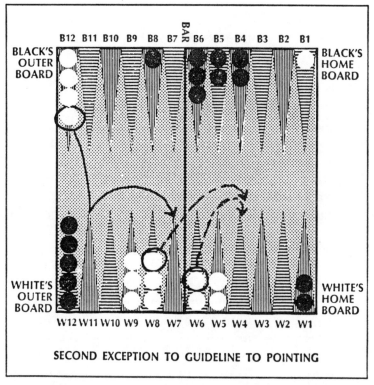

FIGURE 49

SECOND EXCEPTION TO GUIDELINE TO POINTING

each hit each other four times, your chances of coming off the bar the first roll every time are 32%; his are 62%.

Still, we recommend the daring move. We would not consider moving our back man to B3, though, where black can hit him with 2, 5, or 10, twenty-five rolls, without giving up a point. Since he has the better home board, he would welcome a blot-hitting contest.

As the game develops there are fewer pat moves, so you must weigh the various alternatives, as just discussed. But now back to our central theme: You can take chances in your outer board, for you are unlikely to be hit and the rewards are great if you are not. Each new builder increases your chances of making a valuable point on your next roll.

DEFENSIVE TACTICS

What defense do you have against your opponent taking liberties in *his* outer board?

- Run with any appropriate roll: 6-5, 6-4, or even 6-3 and 6-2, if you can get past his blot. But do not stop short, for that would give him two direct shots at your runner.
- Split your back men with 5-1, 4-1, and 2-1 rolls. That doubles your chances of hitting any blot he exposes in the outer board or making a higher point in his home board.
- Make a partial run to B7 with a 6 roll—generally 6-2 or 6-3— if you cannot get past his blot. You lose your gamble when he points on your blot, but you have fourteen ways to bump back if he has to leave a blot there himself.
- Keep him off balance by bringing in builders, hitting his blots, and making points on your side of the table. These are offensive tactics, while all the foregoing were defensive in nature.
- Lastly, when you can make his 5 point you deprive him of his sanctuary, for you will have a direct—not a combination— shot at all the open points in his outer board (remember you already own B12). Then, truly, his outer board becomes your hunting ground.

SAMPLE GAME

Isolated positions distort the flavor of the game and fail to show how individual moves combine into a plan and how one move counters another. Therefore, the following sample game is presented to provide a better perspective. Follow the moves on the board in back. First, all the rolls will be listed without comment to enable you to make your own decisions. Choose black's moves as well; this will double the benefit of the exercise and sharpen your awareness of the effect of an opponent's play on your own. Do not peek at the next roll until you have decided on the current one, for you would not have that opportunity in a real game, unless you are clairvoyant.

White wins the opening roll:

	White	Black
1.	3-1	6-3
2.	4-3	6-4
3.	double 6s	6-2
4.	4-3	5-4
5.	3-2	6-1
6.	4-2	2-1

If you have arrived at the position in Figure 50, take a bow; you have played winning backgammon from both sides of the table!

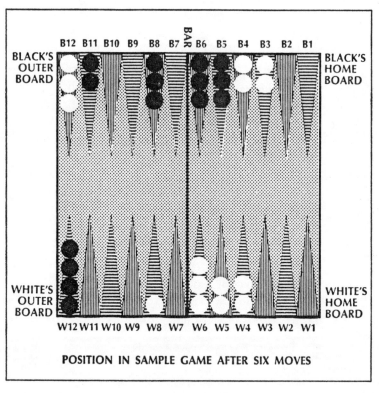

FIGURE 50

POSITION IN SAMPLE GAME AFTER SIX MOVES

Since there were twelve opportunities to go astray, however, it is most unlikely that your position matches ours. So let us explain how and why we reached this position. First, the rolls above were actually thrown at random, but two rolls were discarded because they tended to slow down the tempo. In other words, this sample game was not contrived, only altered slightly.

1. WHITE: 3-1. The classic opening move, making the 5 point (W8-W5, W6-W5).

   BLACK: 6-3. Ordinarily a build-and-run move (B1-B7, W12-B10). In this position, however, white is beginning to restrict black's back men, so black runs all the way (W1-W10).

2. WHITE: 4-3. Hitting the blot on W10 (B12-W10x*) and bringing in another builder (B12-W9). The same move white would ordinarily make pays a dividend of a hit this time.

   BLACK: 6-4. (Bar-W10x). A return hit at the same spot. Black must come off the bar on W4, since W6 is blocked. He continues on to W10 for two reasons: (1) to hit the blot, usually the stand-out move and (2) since he has no other good 6 move.

3. WHITE: double 6s. White cannot come in! It is heartbreaking to roll the highest number and be unable to use it. That is another reason to hit early and often: once in thirty-six rolls your opponent will waste double 6s with his man on the bar.

   BLACK: 6-2. Hits the blot on W9 (W1-W9x). As lucky a roll as the previous one was unlucky. Black does not mind leaving blots outside his home board, since white's entire next roll (except a double) must be used to bring in the two men from the bar.

4. WHITE: 4-3. No choice. Both men must be brought in

---

* In the shorthand for moves used in this book, "x" indicates a hit, in contrast to a move to an unoccupied point or to one on which at least one man of the same color is resting.

(Bar-B3, Bar-B4). White is lucky at that, for any roll with a 6 (eleven possibilities) would bring in only one man, leaving the other on the bar.

BLACK: 5-4. The difference in the dice is 1, just as is the difference between the blots on W9 and W10, so these two men are moved to make a point at B11.

5. WHITE: 3-2. White has a choice of shoring up his position in black's home board (B1-B4, B1-B3) or of making just one point there, the larger for more fire-power (B1-B4) and dropping a blot on W4 (W6-W4), hoping to cover shortly. The first move is purely defensive, so we prefer the alternative of building our own board in anticipation of a hit.

    BLACK: 6-1. Do not make the bar point. Make the 5 point instead (B11-B5, B6-B5). That is the key point in the home board, even more vital here since white has four men who could converge on it.

6. WHITE: 4-2. A handy roll that covers both blots (B1-B3, W8-W4). This secures the back men and provides two shots at incoming black men. Meanwhile, you are building a good board from W6 downward so you will have a reception committee ready for any blot you can hit. This forces black to play more cautiously.

    BLACK: 2-1. (W12-B11, B6-B5). Black immediately covers the blot. The 1 move is more than a temporizing action, for it stations a builder where none was before. A 3/3 pattern on adjoining points is almost always superior to 4/2, since both points can now spare a builder to make a new point.

This is how the position in Figure 50 was reached.

WHO'S AHEAD

One of backgammon's paradoxes is the difficulty of determining by inspection who is leading in the game. Yet some intelligent determination is required for guiding future strategy and deciding whether to double or accept a double.

With a clear lead you should probably double (more on the pitfalls and psychology of doubling appears in Chapter VII and play cautiously to limit the chances of an embarrassing hit. You try to bring your men homeward with the least possible risk. Assuming even luck in the throws of the dice, you should be able to bear your men off first and win.

An entirely different strategy applies when you judge that you have fallen behind. Then you must take risks to catch up. You hang back with some of your men, hoping they will get a shot at a blot. As a consequence, your men may be blocked and you may even be gammoned. But short of conceding the game outright, this is your only means of catching up.

Should you succeed in securing a point at B5 or B4, you have a reasonable hope of a direct shot. Meanwhile, you build up your home board and adjacent points, so that if a hit materializes, that man will have difficulty getting off the bar and escaping homeward.

Backgammon is not a wholesale hunting expedition. One man trapped in the opponent's home board can cost the game. Eventually that man must be granted an exit visa, but only after the opponent has brought in all his men and is ready to bear off. Let's assume the opponent is you, white. Assume that the trapped man is on W1 and black is fortunate enough to roll a 6 immediately after you vacate W7, leaving him a chance to run. The escapee must travel 18 spaces to get home—on the average, two-and-a-half rolls of the dice. By that time you will have borne off four or five men. Black therefore needs two doubles—assuming you do not roll any—just to catch up. In short, trapping a man in the end game creates a commanding lead. Black, realizing this, will probably elect to keep the *trailer* back until the last possible moment for a chance of a shot. Then a hit reverses the situation: your man is stuck on the bar or trapped in black's home court. Of course, by then you have probably borne off several men and may survive to win the game anyway. Or you may not. Every backgammon buff has heard the story—or has been the victim—of a game in which one player bore off fourteen of his men, then suffered a hit, and eventually lost the game.

CONTACT

Backgammon games seesaw constantly. What seemed a brilliant move a few rolls back can quickly turn into a calamity. Therefore, the savvy player leaves himself in fluid position, ready to run when fortune favors, able to stay back when fortune frowns.

In other words, he maintains *contact*. Whenever there is some chance of a hit, there is contact. As soon as all of your men get past all of black's, there is no possibility of a hit. Then contact has been lost.

In Figure 51 there is contact. White's men on B10 and B12 must ultimately make a run to get past black's men on W12 and W7. Likewise black's men must negotiate their way past white's blocked points. The game is still fluid and a good throw by either player could decide the issue. Doubles would be particularly welcome, for they are the only rolls that bring foward a blocked point intact.

In the diagramed position (Figure 51), black has the advantage, for his men on B9 and B8 provide him with more alternate moves before he need run with the men still in contact. The player who must first move the men in contact suffers a disadvantage, for his opponent will get at least one direct shot, in all likelihood. Note that if white now rolls a 6, he has no choice but to move a man from B10. A 6-1 roll is particularly embarrassing, since white cannot bring a man from B10 past black's point on W7: he must therefore permit two direct shots and one combined one (from W7 to B10, or to B11 if white moves the 1 from B10 to B11). Double 6s would bring the men on B10 safely home. 6-4 and 6-3

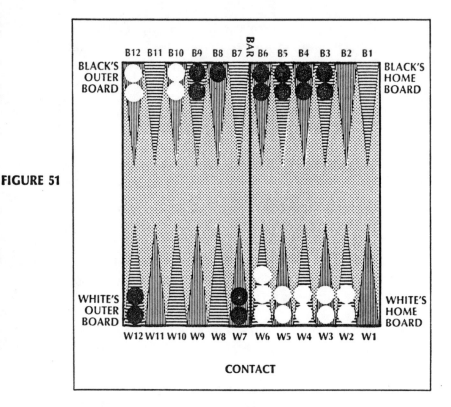

FIGURE 51

CONTACT

would get one man from B10 home and leave a direct and combined shot on the other. Better than those two rolls is 6-2, permitting only one direct shot, since the second man on B10 finds safety at B12.

In fact, white should be thankful for any 2 roll—for it brings one man to temporary safety at B12. Therefore, white should begin his run with 5-2, 4-2, even 2-1; 3-2, though, is a headache, as the 3 cannot be played from B10. White does better to move an *interior man* or two from W6 or below.

Incidentally, how do you play the embarrassing 6-1 roll in this position? No choice on the 6, since your mid men cannot be moved either 1 or 6. So you advance a man from B10 to W9. What about the 1? (W9-W8)? or (B10-B11)? Most players agonize briefly or look heavenward for inspiration, yet there is just one correct play. (B10-B11). Either way, you leave two direct shots from W7 and W12, but our play telescopes the two into just one number on the dice—2—since each blot is 2 spaces away from the men threatening him. Try it the other way—B10 and W8— and black can hit the first blot with any 1 and the second with any 3—twenty possible rolls, versus twelve our way. (Either play opens up, in addition, four unavoidable combined shots.)

Note well this pointer: when two direct shots are inevitable, try to position them equally from their potential captors.

Take the same position but imagine that the three men on W6 are further forward, so you cannot move a 5 within your home board. How do you then play a 5-1? Again, you can reduce the two direct shots to one (B10-W10) for the 5, and waste the 1 with a move in your home board. Each blot is then 3 spaces away from an enemy point.

The general rule in running from two blocked points in the end game is to move first off the further point. As was shown with a roll of 2, the nearer point can sometimes accommodate the *straggler* safely, but the reverse is impossible. Secondly, more rolls can get the men on the nearer point safely home—or with minimum exposure—since they have a shorter distance to travel.

More on contact: In theory, there is still contact in Figure 52, but as a practical matter, contact has been lost. Each player will rush his men homeward, being careful not to leave a blot on the other's 12 point. The only awkward roll is a 1; all others get both mid men easily past their counterparts.

How, then, should white play a 4-1 roll? You cannot bring in both mid men, and it is foolhardy to bring in just one and leave the other as a target. So far so good, but there is a second trap. Pointing on W3 (W8-W3) is tempting, but what if the fates next hand you a 6-1 roll? You must then move one mid man—it is the only playable 6 left—but cannot move the other. You are in the precise dangerous position you hoped to avoid: black needs only a 1 to hit your blot and probably win the game.

You could easily have prevented this debacle by making an interior move, such as (W6-W2, W5-W4), thereby keeping you in reserve a playable 6 from W8. Ordinarily, in a running game you bring your men into your home board as quickly as possible, but this situation is an exception.

FIGURE 52

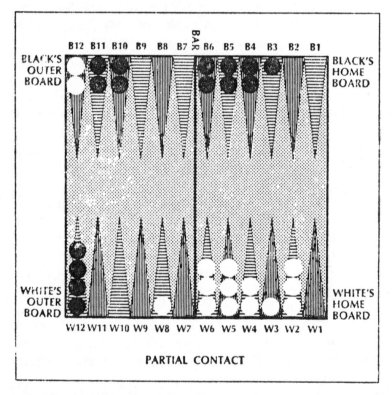

PARTIAL CONTACT

THE RUNNING GAME

Once contact is lost, you are in a running game. Each player runs for all he is worth, wasting not a single pip on the dice. The sooner all your men reach your home board, the sooner you can start bearing them off. Preferably, you would distribute your men evenly among all six home points, for then you are sure to bear off at least four men on the first two rolls. Contrariwise, when all your men are piled up on, say, the 5 and 6 points, a 1, 2, 3, or 4 on a die prevents you from bearing off a man.

But first things first: you cannot bear off even a single man until they are all home, so your first concern is to bring them home. Thus in Figure 53, you roll 4-1 and think wistfully about evening out your board (W6-W2, W4-W3), but you cannot afford such an indulgence. Instead, bring in your men on W10 and W7 to W6, so you can begin to bear off on your next roll.

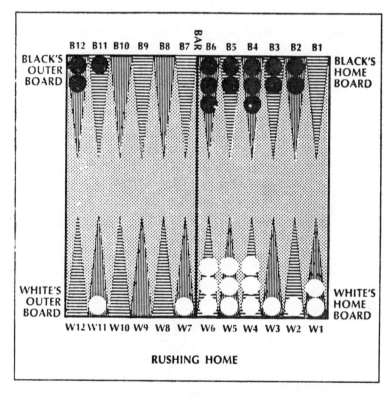

FIGURE 53

In fairness, few players make the error of tarrying with the last few men in their outer board, but many accidently slow themselves down when they have men further out.

Stinginess becomes a virtue in the running game. You should look for full value for each of your rolls. Do not squander a 6 roll to bring in a man just 1 space away. You will begrudge those wasted 5 pips if you next roll a small number.

The most economical approach is to advance a man from one board to the next on each number on a die whenever possible. Then he can progress one board further on a 6 roll, at worst. This rule ensures the most efficient use of the rolls, that is, wastes the fewest pips.

With that rule in mind, how would you play a 3-2 roll in Figure 54? Do not waste the entire roll to bring in the man from W10. In preference, advance your two other trailers to your outer board (B10-W12, B11-W12).

FIGURE 54

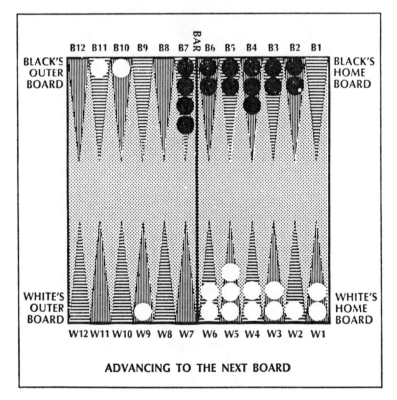

ADVANCING TO THE NEXT BOARD

All rules have exceptions. In Figure 52 we recommended that you move two men within your home board rather than bring in the man on W8. Since you are far ahead in the running game, you can afford an insurance premium against a 1.7% chance (2/36, odds of your rolling 6-1, times 11/36, odds of black rolling a 1 to hit). If the running game were not so one-sided, you should bring in the man from W8 immediately without a second thought about the remoteness of a hit at B12.

THE RUNNING COUNT

Returning to our sample game (Figure 50, repeated for convenience), who is ahead? A more germane question might be:

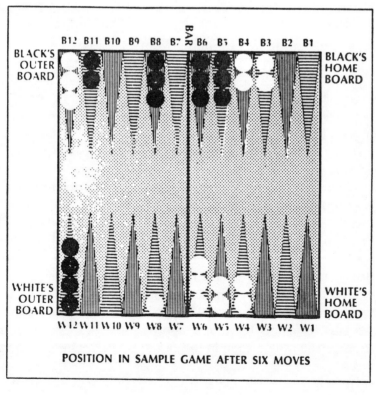

FIGURE 50 (Repeated)

POSITION IN SAMPLE GAME AFTER SIX MOVES

"How can you tell?" One·method is to *count the position*—determine the total number of spaces your men must travel before all are borne off. The total is your *running count*. Determine black's running count in the same way and then compare. Whoever has the smaller running count is ahead.

Starting with your men in the home board, you count 4 each for the two men on W4, or 8 total; 5 each for the two men on W5, or 10 total; 6 each for the three men on W6, or 18 total. Your total home board count is therefore 36. In your outer board you have 8 points (one man on W8) for a running count total of 44 on your side of the table. On the other side you cannot use the point number, for that measures *black's* distance from point zero, not yours. Your men on B12 actually must move 13 spaces before they are borne off; your men on B4, 21 each. The quickest way to compute the count on the opposite side of the table is to subtract the point number from 25. Thus, 25 minus B12 = 13, times 3 men equals 39, bringing our count up to 83.

Now to black's home board: 25 minus B4 = 21 times 2 men equals 42. Similarly, with the two men on B3: 25 minus B3 = 22 times 2 = 44. Toting up all the figures, we get a total of 169 spaces to travel before all our men are off the board. We have actually *lost* ground since the game began! In the starting position we anticipated a trip of 167 spaces.

There is no mistake. The apparent discrepancy can be checked out if you care to take the trouble. On your six rolls of the dice your effective total was 29, excluding the double 6s you could not move when you had a man on the bar. But you were set back by hits on your men at W10 and W9. These men had already traveled 15 and 16 spaces respectively toward home (another application of the 25 key figure: 25 − W10 = 15), so the two hits cost you 31 spaces. The total of 29 on the dice less 31 for the loss from hits leave you minus 2 spaces. Nobody bothers to reconcile the position in this fashion, but it is helpful to know it can be done.

In any event, white has a trip of 169 spaces ahead of him.

Counting black's position in the same way reveals his running count to be 131. We trail by the difference—38 spaces, or approximately five rolls of the dice (the average roll being 8 1/6*). Whoever has the higher running count actually trails in the game, as he has further to go.

This process involves a good deal of tabulating. An easier approach is to keep track of just the difference as you go along, offsetting equivalent positions. For example, each player has three men on his 6 point, so there is no difference there. Black has one more man on his 5 point than we, so that counts 5 against him, but we have a total of 8 points for W4. Up to this stage we trail by 3 (5 minus 8). White pulls temporarily ahead at the 8 point, where he picks up 16 points, for a net plus of 13. He adds 13 more at the 12 point, for a cumulative total of 26. Black's two men on B11 swell the total by 22, to 48. Then, alas, our four men in black's home board dissipate the lead and throw us into the minus column: 48 minus 86 equals minus 38.

A still simpler approach is to take a rough count, giving all the men in the same board the same value. Assign 4 points for each of your men in black's home board, 3 for those in his outer board, 2 each in your outer board, 1 in your home board. Under this formula you have a count of 7 in your home board, ·2 in your outer board, 9 in black's outer board, and 16 in black's home board. Or a total of 34. Black's figures, respectively, are

---

* As every craps player can tell you, the average roll of the dice is 7. But since doubles in backgammon count at twice their usual value, the average roll increases correspondingly. To take this into account, add the numbers on the six sides of a dice, double the total, then divide by 36, the number of possible combinations of the dice. That gives you 1 1/6. Add that to the average of "straight dice," 7, and you have 8 1/6. Of course, nobody has ever had a roll of 8 1/6, just as no family boasts 2.7 children. It may console the craps player to know that in backgammon the mode and median remain at 7. (The 8 1/6 figure is technically not just "an average," but a specific kind of average—the arithmetic mean.) That is, more rolls total 7 than any other number; and there are as many totals of the dice smaller than 7 as there are larger than 7. Nothing in the foregoing explanation will improve your backgammon game one whit.

6, 10, and 12, for a total of 28. The difference is 6 with black leading in the race.

To convert this figure into number of turns, merely divide
by 2. So, by this formula, black leads by three rolls, contrasted
with five rolls under the running count system. Obviously the
latter is more accurate, so the reader is forewarned that the
rough count is just that; it does not distinguish among the positions *within the board* of the various men. The distortion is
greater when men are bunched at either end of a board.

Easiest of all is to figure just the net difference with the
rough count. In Figure 50 the inner boards net 1 point minus
for you; in the outer boards you pick up 8; switching over to
the "opposite" outer boards (your men in black's, his in yours),
you gain 3 more. But you lose 16 points for your four men in
black's home board, so you trail by 6—the same result derived
earlier.

Usually inspection alone substitutes admirably for the
count. In Figure 50 you observe your four men in black's home
board and look in vain for any of his in yours. His "missing"
four men rest much closer to their home (B8 and B11), while
the rest of the position is about equal. Comparing just the eight
dislocated men—four of each color—you conclude sadly that
yours have a trip of 86 spaces ahead, while black's must travel
only 46. The difference, 40 spaces, is about five rolls.

And yet another system: We have experimented with keeping
a net count of the dice as the game progresses so we need never
stop to count. Easy enough when there is no hit: whoever rolls
the better dice leads by the margin between the totals. For each
hit, however, you must pause a few seconds to make an adjust-
ment: compute the distance already traveled by the man sent
to the bar and charge it against the player who suffered the hit.

The calculations are hardly worth the trouble, particularly
since you require an accurate count only a few times during a
game. Besides, the effort interferes with one's concentration
or else slows up the game.

Nonetheless, for those quick with figures, here is a short example: in the game we played out through six moves (to the position on Figure 50) white was ahead 2 pips after his second roll. Black's second roll put him in the lead by 8, plus the value of the hit: the man at W10 was 15 steps from the starting line, so 15 plus 8 produces black's current lead of 23 spaces.

ADVANTAGE OF THE ROLL

Usually you count the position at your turn, before you cast the dice if you are contemplating a double, after if you are deciding on your tactics. Either way, you have a built-in advantage. Your current roll adds to your lead, or reduces your deficit. If you forget this factor, nothing is lost. A hidden safety factor is working in your favor, that's all.

But in judging whether to accept a double, you should be conscious of the roll factor and adjust for it. Since your opponent is about to roll, add 8 points—an average roll—to his lead and decide whether the new total warrants acceptance of the double.

To restate: when you are about to roll, you are 8 points to the good; when your opponent picks up the dice, he is 8 points better off. Perhaps obvious, but many experienced players seem unaware of the distinction.

COUNTING ROLLS

In the last stages of a running game, it is easier and more accurate to count the number of rolls to your objective, rather than to determine the running count. In Figure 55 the running count shows no advantage, yet your position is superior. Two rolls of the dice will surely bring in all your men to your home board, but black needs two rolls of 7 or better to accomplish the same result. Should he roll, say, 6-2 and 5-1, for an *average* of 7, he will require another half a roll before he can start bearing off.

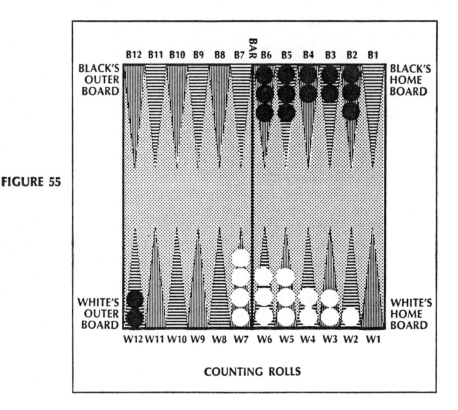

FIGURE 55

B12 B11 B10 B9 B8 B7 BAR B6 B5 B4 B3 B2 B1

BLACK'S OUTER BOARD

BLACK'S HOME BOARD

WHITE'S OUTER BOARD

WHITE'S HOME BOARD

W12 W11 W10 W9 W8 W7 W6 W5 W4 W3 W2 W1

COUNTING ROLLS

SAMPLE GAME RESUMED

Earlier we observed that tactics change as the lead shifts, as we see as we return to our sample game (Figure 50, page 99).

7. WHITE: 6-5. Should he run with a back man? Bring in a mid man? Build his board?

To make an intelligent decision white must count the position. He concludes that he is five rolls behind—actually four, since it is his turn. White will need four doubles to catch up, assuming black rolls none. Clearly too much to expect. Is there an alternative? Yes, keep both points at B3 and B4, waiting for a two-pronged shot at a black blot in his outer board. Having reached that decision, white has an easy move (W8-W3,

B12-W7). Now a 3 or 4 roll will cover the blot on W3 for a four-point board. The new position is illustrated in Figure 56.

BLACK: 6-4. He could play safe temporarily (B8-B2, B6-B2) but that merely postpones facing up to his problem—few combinations of the dice will bring in his mid men without uncovering a blot. 6-1 would be perfect, pointing at B7; any 2, 5, 7, 8, 11, or 12 will bring one mid man to safety. Apparently plenty of chances, but all but 6-1 bring in one mid man at a time. Eventually black may have to leave a blot at W12 open to a hit on a 1 roll from B12. By that time white's home board will be stronger and black will not relish a trip to the bar. Of course, black can hope to wait out the position, calculating that white will have to vacate B12 before black leaves a blot at W12.

Weighing the risks, black should make the bolder move (W12-B7, B11-B7), making his bar point, filling a gap, constructing four consecutive blocked points. This forward-looking move serves several purposes:

- One additional safe resting place is available for black's mid men.
- A more complete block has been set up against white's men at B3 and B4.
- The options of these men are restricted: only a 6 can move a man from B3, for he can no longer touch down on a 4 roll; nor can the men on B4 move a 3 roll.
- Temporizing moves are preserved in case black rolls badly: 6 from B8, 5 or 4 from B6, 3 or 4 from B5.

What of the disadvantages? The blot left at B11 is open to six combination shots. If hit, he has three open points in white's home board on which to reenter—twenty-seven rolls.

Yet our recommended move will stick in the craw of many players. "Why leave a blot when you do not have to?" Simply because you will probably have to leave a more dangerous one later. In general, the player in the lead cannot afford to hang back, since his opponent is still further back and can wait him out. That creates a situation where whoever makes the first hit takes a commanding lead. Since black is now far ahead, he does not want to play that waiting game.

Give white full marks, though. By maintaining three points on black's side of the table he has forced black's hand. Now he has the two-pronged shot he hoped for. Unfortunately, they add up to only six combinations on the dice, because of the four intervening blocked points. Still, that is better than no shot at all.

8.   WHITE: 6-4. White misses and has four choices:

- Run with a back man (B4-W11). No good, for we ruled out the running tactic after we determined that we were five rolls behind.
- Bring in both mid men (B12-W7, B12-W9). That relieves the direct pressure on W12, allowing black to bring in one mid man at a time eventually exposing a blot at W12. But our guns at B3 and B4 are barely within range.
- Move in the home board (W7-W1, W6-W2), leaving three blots. We will need a 1 or 2 roll to cover, meanwhile surrendering our good chances to cover at W3. Clearly not a progressive move. Moreover, black can play wide open on his next turn, since our home board is so porous. Granted white might hit and have a 1 or 2 on the other die; that would leave but one blot in white's home board and that is also wishful thinking.
- Send in one mid man to cover at W3 (B12-W3), exposing a blot at B12. By elimination, this is the best move. White will have a four-point board, two builders at W6 and W7 ready to make an additional point, and a mid man as sentinel to keep black's mid men honest. The sole drawback is the blot uncovered at B12. No tragedy if hit, though. A fifth man back will not hurt white's chances. He will have four open points on which to come in, two of which are safe ports. More to the issue, white would welcome an opportunity to

slow down his game; otherwise after a couple moves he will either be forced to weaken his home board or give up a point in black's home board.

This time it is white who unnecessarily but wisely leaves a blot:
BLACK: 6-5. Easy (B12-B7, B11-B6), removing the blot, leaving builders and reserve moves on four successive points.

9. WHITE: 5-4. A perfect roll for a change, but check the Guideline to Pointing (p. 94) before reading further ... The difference in the dice is 1, so white can point on W2 (W7-W2, W6-W2) for a five-point board. But he is running out of available moves and time grows short.
BLACK: 5-2. Black stalls (B8-B1), hoping that by the time he must move his mid men, white's position will have deteriorated.

10. WHITE: 6-3. White reluctantly vacates B12 and uses up his last surplus move (B12-W4). The alternative (B3-B12) would leave a blot at B3, subject to a hit-and-cover (at B1) with 5-2, 4-2, 3-2, or double 2s—seven rolls of the dice. Looking ahead, white sees no reason to chance the hit, as he can run with a 5 or 6 on his next turn or move rolls of 4 or less within his home board.
BLACK: 4-2. (B7-B1). Still temporizing, covering the blot meanwhile.

11. WHITE: 4-1. (W5-W1) (W4-W3). White's board starts to totter, but he allows for the most reasonable chances: 5-1 or 2-1 would cover at W5 and W1 for a five-point board; any 5, 4, 2, or 1 will cover one point.
BLACK: 4-3. An excellent roll, furthering the temporizing game, while making a new point past white (B6-B2, B5-B2).

12. WHITE: Double 4s. Horrendous. White is reduced to a four-point board (two from W6-W2, W5-W1, the

fourth 4 is unplayable).

BLACK: 6-2. Still playing it safe (B8-B6, B8-B2). Sending in one mid man would leave only six combination shots at the blot left on W12, but there is no reason to run even that risk.

13. WHITE: 6-3. Forced to run to move the 6 (B3-B12).

BLACK: 6-3. No way to play this safely, so black chooses the best move of hitting the blot (B6-B3x) and bringing in one mid man (W12-B7). Thus black extracts a high price for leaving a blot: white must waste a half-roll and may not be able to come off the bar for a turn or two. Generally it is advantageous to hit when you must leave a blot open to a direct shot in any event. In this case, black must leave two blots; leaving the second one at B7 (B7-B1) is a mite safer—only a 4-3 roll will hit there. However, looking ahead, black wisely decides to hold the point at B7 as a safe port for his mid men, and so he moves one mid man off, even though the blot left at W12 can be hit with either a 4-1 or 3-1 roll.

14. WHITE: 5-1. White misses his second chance for a hit, his first direct shot. However, he is happy to stay on the bar, for it slows down his game and preserves his home board.

BLACK: 6-5. Infuriating. This is one of three possible rolls (double 6s is the other) that will not cover or move the blot at B3. Black has nothing better to do than run safely with his remaining mid man (B12-B2).

15. WHITE: 6-1. Again white misses—probably his last chance at a hit for some time.

BLACK: 4-1. Finally covers the blot (B7-B3) and brings in a man (B7-B6). This opens up an unnecessary blot at B7 vulnerable to only two rolls (4-3)—a negligible risk as against black's chance for a gammon if he rushes ahead. (See Chapter VII for a shortcut formula for evaluating gammon possibilities.)

16. WHITE: 5-4. Out at last (Bar-B4) and running for home (B4-B9.) Since only two men are needed to hold the point at B4, white hurries to get his two trailers into his home board.

BLACK: 4-3. (B7-B3). Black gets his last man home and bears off one man (B3). The game is practically over but black will not relax until he has borne off his six men on B5 and B6 or moved them past white's point.

REVIEW OF THE SAMPLE GAME

White's hit at W10 on his second turn put him ahead in the running game and gave him a positional advantage as well, since he had made his 5 point and had two builders deployed. Black's subsequent two hits swung the balance in his favor and extricated his two back men, who shortly pointed on B11. Meanwhile, white threw the one roll that could cost him a turn and leave his men on the bar. This gave black time to consolidate and a significant lead, as verified by figuring the running count.

Still, black had few safe ports for his mid men. He took a calculated risk to make his bar point, easing his problem considerably. Black then became an overwhelming favorite. Nonetheless, white got a combination shot from two outposts and later two direct shots, while he had a decent home board. He missed both times and was never given another chance.

Most backgammon games seesaw back and forth more than this one. One fortuitous or calamitous roll of the dice changes the course of the game—until the next surprise. The casual player ascribes victory to the vagaries of the dice, unaware that the thoughtful player has protected himself, insofar as possible, against difficult combinations.

In fact, this provides one standard of evaluating a position. Determine how many rolls of the dice work out favorably, how many unfavorably, and how many are neutral. This is an especially valuable criterion when contemplating a double *on the come,* in expectation of a good roll favored by the odds. The conservative player rarely uses this tactic, preferring to be certain of the good roll, planning to double *after* it arrives. A bird in hand and all that. But the bird had flown the coop, the double is declined. An aggressive player forces the issue before the crucial throw. If the double is accepted, the doubler has the odds on his side; if it is declined, the doubler has collected insurance against one of the disappointing combinations of the dice.

In Figure 56 we saw an extreme case. No roll could hurt black. He actually rolled 6-4, one of the better numbers. But before he rolled, what were the probabilities?

- No roll would force black to leave a blot. In that sense, black has an enviable position.
- However, only six rolls safely make a new point in his outer board to serve as a stopover for his mid men. These rolls are 6-1, double 2s, 3s, 4s, 6s.
- Six more rolls (6-4, 4-2, 3-1) enable black to make a point in his outer board at the risk of leaving a blot, which would be subject to seven combined shots.
- The remaining twenty-four rolls bring in a mid man or put black's inner man further forward, but this just postpones the problem—will black be able to bring in all his mid men safely?

Black's prospects should be viewed in the context of white's position. White has fewer moves left before he must run with a back man or move off the higher numbered points in his home board. Therefore, black can afford to stall, and his twenty-four neutral rolls might be considered favorable. Had white been kept on the bar longer, or rolled smaller numbers, he might have been able to keep his men further back, buying time. Then black's twenty-four neutral rolls become more ominous with each succeeding turn.

Certainly we could have created a less involved position, but

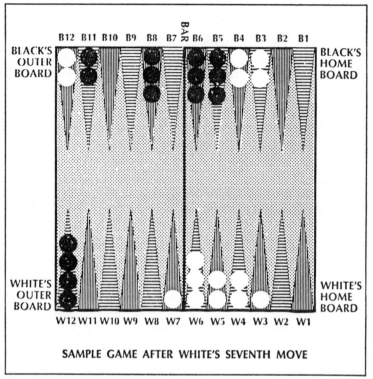

FIGURE 56

B12 B11 B10 B9 B8 B7 BAR B6 B5 B4 B3 B2 B1

BLACK'S OUTER BOARD

BLACK'S HOME BOARD

WHITE'S OUTER BOARD

WHITE'S HOME BOARD

W12 W11 W10 W9 W8 W7 W6 W5 W4 W3 W2 W1

SAMPLE GAME AFTER WHITE'S SEVENTH MOVE

this one actually resulted from random throws of the dice. Moreover, it illuminates a backgammon axiom: many murky positions defy precise analysis; others can be solved only by a computer, but certainly not at the table. All part of the mystery of backgammon.

Nothing has been said about white's favorable rolls. He has virtually none! Oh, double 6s would free all four men from black's home board and narrow the margin. Double 5s and double 4s would bring one back point forward for a better shot at black's men. Three rolls out of thirty-six. White is deployed defensively, so he is condemned to wait for an opening—a shot at a blot. Then, and then only, can he make a meaningful calculation of constructive, neutral, and damaging combinations.

CHAPTER V
Timing

The sample game in the last chapter was never completed. We know only that white needs exceptional dice to pull the game out. Long-term probabilities can be stated with mathematical certainty, but the outcome of a given game—the short term—is in doubt until the very end. In our sample game there is no immutable law against white throwing double 6s three times in a row to win the game, but the odds against him can be stated precisely—one chance in 46,656 (1/36 x 1/36 x 1/36).

The backgammon buff accepts the vagaries, fickleness, and, yes, even the injustice of the dice. In fact, he adapts to them. He keeps his game flexible and is able to switch from a blocking game to a running game, to break off contact or to position his men where his opponent must maneuver to get past.

In the early game the winning backgammon player lets the dice lead him. He makes the move best suited to his roll. Later, he evaluates his chances and chooses his moves accordingly. He may run with a back man, expose a blot to build a better board, keep his men back, solidify his forces, play wide open or close to the vest—all depending upon his evaluation of the position. But he tries to avoid letting the game hinge on one roll of the dice—unless he has long odds in his favor. He improves his chances by banking on a reasonable series of several throws. Therefore he tries to construct a position that is flexible enough to survive an unfortunate roll. Of course, every backgammon player prays for specific rolls, but the expert takes out insurance in the form of a fluid position.

WHEN TO RUN

Figure 57 illustrates a common predicament. White throws 5-3. Does he run from B7 or does he stay? The answer depends upon white's estimate of the position. If he is ahead in the running game, he should bring both men forward from B7. If he is behind, then he should keep his point on B7, build up his board, and wait for a chance at a shot.

Actually white is ahead, so he moves one man safely to B12; the other becomes a blot at B10. Barring doubles, this is the best running roll white is likely to get. By running now, white is exposed to thirteen direct shots (the fourteen usual ones less double 1s, blocked by B12). Observe that white runs with *both* men; to leave a blot at B7 would expose him to direct shots from B8, B9, and W12—any 1, 2, or 6, or twenty-eight combinations.

At this moment white can tolerate a hit, since black has not yet developed a strong board. A few moves later, however, white may be less sanguine about being caught.

The problem in Figure 58 looks similar, but the solution differs. Here white is behind in the running game, so he retains the point at B7, seeking a shot as black's mid men come in. In reply, black may take evasive action that costs him a roll or two. This may be just the edge that white needs to change course and head for home with good rolls.

Fortunately, white has an excellent alternative to running (W8-W3, W6-W3), making the 3 point, improving his board, and further inhibiting black's mid men.

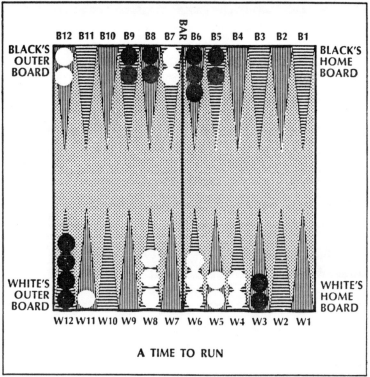

FIGURE 57

A TIME TO RUN

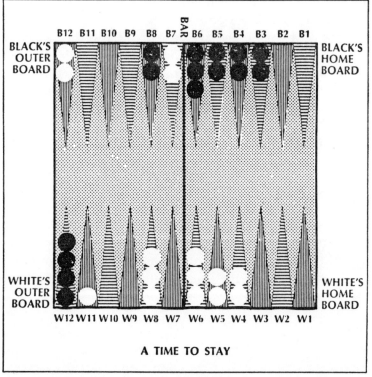

FIGURE 58

A TIME TO STAY

KEY POINTS IN THE END GAME

The aggressive player tries to secure his opponent's 5 point, bar point, or 4 point, in that order of preference. The value of these three stations persists throughout the game. In the late stages they become outposts for shots at the last of the enemy men coming homeward. At the same time, they are quick departure points should you decide to run yourself.

But these three vaunted points are not sinecures. When you are far behind in the running game you may regret relinquishing your hold on B1. At that ultimate stronghold you probably would get a shot or two at black as he bears off. Having advanced to B5 or thereabouts, you may be bypassed. In our sample game white held points at both B3 and B4, yet black sent men behind them, dropping blots on B1 and B2 without risk.

In Figure 57 white's hold on B7 became a drawback when he drew ahead in the running count and chose to flee first. Usually this opens the runner to a direct shot, at the least. But white does worse to tarry, for the timing will continue to favor black as he continues to improve his home board.

In the late game the opponent's 12 point looms more powerful. Once your back men have departed, this is the last way station from which you can command your entire outer board and snipe at the last of black's back men fleeing homeward. When you have men further back, B12 is a convenient resting place for them as they come homeward.

KEEPING FLUID

The pure running game is easy to play and dull to watch. The better dice prevail. Experts, like the veriest tyros, will run full speed when they are ahead in the running count. Until that point, however, they keep their position fluid, they maintain contact. When the dice swing in their favor, or they score a good hit, they try to disengage and run for home.

Figure 59 is a recurring scenario. Black is 22 ahead in the running count. White must play to keep his point at B7, hoping for a shot. Black eventually ran his last back man out to W11. Let's consider how white should play the various rolls:

- Double 6s. This puts you temporarily 2 points ahead in the running count. Another high roll, coupled with a small one by black, would put you ahead, forcing you to move your trailers before black's, probably exposing a blot. Then you

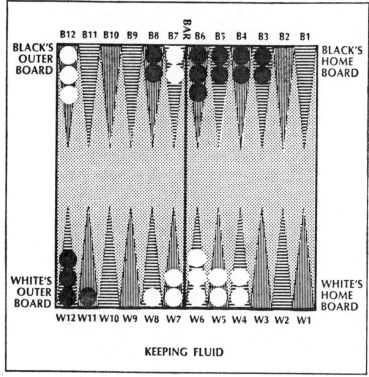

FIGURE 59

KEEPING FLUID

would be grateful to have the point at B12 as a home for your men from B7, so do not give it up now. The situation is still cloudy, so stay fluid. Take a temporizing move: (B12-W1, W8-W2, W7-W1). This retains your point on B12, builds a new point in your home board, brings in a blot at W2 you can cover later, retains a 6 move (from W7) for a subsequent roll should you want to keep your point on B12 for another turn or so.

- Double 5s. Momentarily you are just 2 points behind in the running game—close enough to run yourself and hope for better dice. But we prefer staying back and improving our board (B12-W3, W7-W2, W6-W1).

- 4-3. Hit the blot (B7-W11). Black can hit back with fifteen combinations, a 42% chance, so the odds are with you. Note also, that you are now just 4 points behind in the running count (deduct your 7 on the dice and the 11 spaces the blot had traveled homeward). If black cannot come off the bar, you will go ahead. Even if he does get off on his first roll, but fails to hit you, you have a good blocking network to keep him in. You plan to bring your blot on B7 to safety and improve your home board.

- 5-2. Hit (B12-W11) but do not advance from B7. Not because it is too risky—fifteen adverse combinations can hit you, as above—but because you have a better move: (B12-W8), giving you five points toward a prime. You take daring risks to make a prime, for it practically ensures the game, unless you break your prime too soon, or your opponent constructs one that outlasts yours.

- 3-2. Hit (B12-W11) and cover the blot (W11-W8) for your fifth point toward a prime.

- 6-2, 4-2, or 2-1. Hit with the 2 (B12-W11) and advance the same man the count on the other die.

- Double 2s. Hit (B12-W11) and advance that man and another mid man to point on B9. Now you need only a 6 to cover the blot at B7 for a prime.

- All other rolls maintain the status quo: black leads in the running count, so you hold both points at B12 and B7, meanwhile building your board and waiting for black to move off first to leave you a shot.

ONE LAST CHANCE

No matter how far behind you are in the running count, there is always a chance to recover if you get one last shot. What could be more hopeless than white's position in Figure 60? If

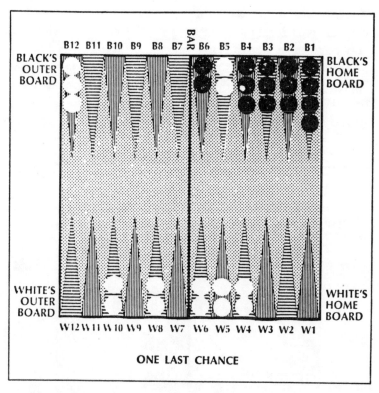

FIGURE 60

ONE LAST CHANCE

you trouble to figure the running count—and no self-respecting person in white's seat should—you are 102 points behind, and it is black's roll to boot. Eureka! Black rolls a 6-1 (5-1 would be equally gratifying) and has a forced move—bearing off a man from B6. But your point at B5 thwarts him from moving the other man at B6 past you, so you have a shot. Any 1 roll will do it and a hit will probably win the game for you. Even though you have only a 3-point board, his trailer will have the devil's own time working past your nine men strategically placed around the table. You keep hitting him while building more points in your home board. Each time he finds it more difficult to run. Eventually you may be able to construct a prime or closed board.

Since we referred to the running count so frequently, you may be wondering how a lead of 102 could possibly dwindle and become a deficit. First off, each hit reduces black's lead. In addition, black loses some rolls and wastes part of others. In Figure 61, we have progressed several rolls from the last position. White hit black's blot, hit him again as he came out. Black stayed on the bar two turns, so those two rolls do not affect his

FIGURE 61

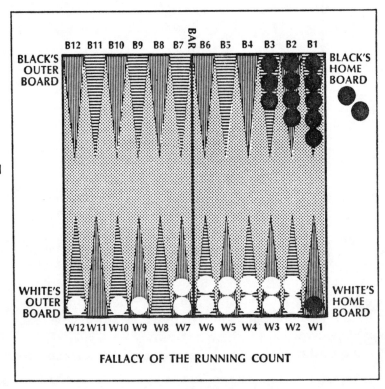

FALLACY OF THE RUNNING COUNT

running count. In the current position black cannot move any number but a 1 or 2, so whatever else he rolls will not lower his running count. Eventually black will be unable to move even a 1, so his running count will remain constant while each of your rolls reduces yours.

Even in this position, where it is obvious that black trails badly, he still leads in the running count, 85 to 46. The gap will narrow as black cannot move while white utilizes his full role each time. Eventually white will take the lead in the running count, which will finally catch up to the reality of the end game. The lesson: when a man is trapped in his opponent's home board, ignore the running count entirely. One look at the trapped man and you know who will win.

THE BACK GAME

Position and timing determine the outcome of most well-played backgammon games. Rarely can a player escape a hit or two during an entire game. When the hit occurs in the late stages and the opponent has a good board, that single hit often decides the game. Yet, the running count as we have seen, may be lopsided in the other direction.

Nowhere is this better demonstrated than in the *back game*. In Figure 62 white has fallen far behind, having been hit several times and then failing—or never trying—to bring his back men out. However, white has managed to secure two points in black's home board and these can prove troublesome.

Black managed to bring in all his men without leaving a blot and has borne off two men. However, he has had to maneuver around white's two blocked points and his options on each roll were severely limited. In this position black has a forced move for any 3, 5, or 6 and only two ways to move a 2 or a 4. Fifteen combinations of the dice will open a blot at B5, black's Achilles heel, which white can hit with twenty possible rolls. And, of course, after a hit, white is a favorite to win the game. Therefore, white's immediate chances are 15/36 x 20/36, or 23%, not

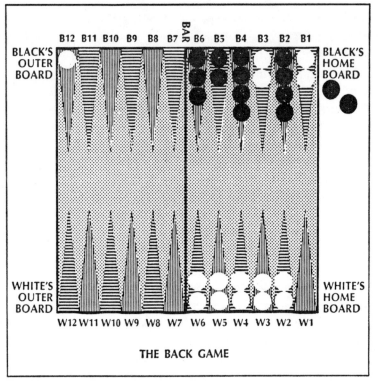

FIGURE 62

THE BACK GAME

bad for a "hopeless game."

Assume black survives his turn with a 5-1 roll, bearing off one man from B5 and covering the blot (B6-B5). Now he has two men on B5 and B6, hence two weak links in the chain. White rolls a 4-2 and advances his mid man (B12-W7).

Black's prospects at his next turn are slightly better— twenty-four safe combinations, but with one important difference: four of the unsafe combinations (6-5 and 6-3) force black to leave two blots, on B6 and B5. In that event, white becomes a favorite to win the game, for thirty-two combinations of the dice will hit the blot—any 2, 3, 4, or 5. Put another way, only double 1s and 6s and 6-1 will miss.

However, black rolls safely—double 5s, a forced move (two

men borne off from B5, the remaining two 5s being unplayable), and white rolls 2-1 (W7-W4). Black's situation is still precarious; he has twenty-two safe rolls.

THE MYSTIQUE OF THE BACK GAME

The back game has revolutionized modern backgammon, providing a means of snatching victory from a hopeless situation. For the beginner to seek situations where he can test this new-found stratagem would be sheer folly, however.

A few admonitions about the back game are in order:

- In a well-played back game both players have about an equal chance to win. That accounts for the mystique; who can resist the lure of retrieving a lost cause?
- However, the player who goes into a back game usually pays double when he loses—that is, he suffers a gammon. If he runs with some of his back men, he no longer has a true back game; if he stays and fails to hit, he lacks the time to get home and bear a man off.
- Thus, even though you have an even chance to win a particular back game from the trailing position, the long-term odds are 2 to 1 against you. Each game you win nets you 1 unit; the games you lose cost 2 units each.
- Therefore, nobody in a serious game sets out from the beginning deliberately to play a back game. The position evolves after one player has been hit several times and falls far behind in the running count. He then elects to retreat into a back game by trying to secure two points in his adversary's home board. Careful preparation precedes a good back-game position, as you shall soon see.

In one sense, back games just "happen," for one player falls so far behind that the back game is his only salvation. In another sense, a back game is "prepared," since the trailing player must begin to construct the final position long before it matures.

The ingredients of a good back game are:

- Two points held in the opponent's home board, preferably the lower ones. B1/B3 and B1/B2 are the classic positions in that order. Black can bypass the higher numbered points with less difficulty, thereby bringing some men to safety. Ideally, the two points you hold should be adjoining or two spaces apart, so that when a blot opens up, both points can zero in on it.
- Timing. In a back game you must be prepared to "wait it out." You may not get a shot for several rolls, if at all. Meanwhile, you must move the rolls on your dice entirely with your remaining eleven men. Therefore you must try to keep men back in the two outer boards—and preferably a fifth man on one of your points in black's home board—to consume the numbers on the dice without impairing your home board. The longer you can wait, the better your chances.

In Figure 62 time was running out for white. His sole man in the outer boards could travel only 12 spaces before his limit was reached. An extra man in the outer boards could buy a couple of rolls, which might prove crucial.

In Figure 63 white seems to have his men scattered aimlessly around the board, but actually he is in excellent shape for the forthcoming back game. His four men in the outer boards are worth 24 pips on the dice, about three rolls. Note well the third man on B3. He can begin his trip home as soon as black vacates B9—probably in a couple of rolls—and white rolls a 6. That will consume another 16 pips on the dice to get to W6 and leave a safety margin of 5 pips to W1. That amounts to almost three more rolls of the dice. All told, white has about six turns before all eleven men are deployed in his home board—six turns in which to hit a blot black may be forced to leave.

The fifth man in black's home board is one of the keys to a good back game. He is placed as far back as possible to lengthen the trip homeward and buy time, yet far enough forward to be able to get out when the opportunity arises.

Preparing for the back game is analogous to the philosophy

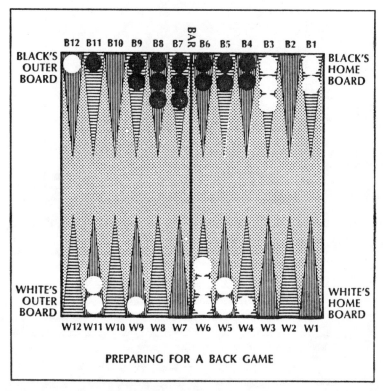

FIGURE 63

PREPARING FOR A BACK GAME

of some professional football coaches, who bring their men along slowly in spring practice, so they do not reach their peak until midseason. In the back game you prepare slowly so that your board will mature just as black feels the pinch.

After a few rolls the position might be as in Figure 64. Note how white's apparent chaos has coalesced into the makings of a good board. Black now rolls a 6-5 and must leave a blot (B8-B2, B7-B2). However, white fails to hit and a few turns later we have this position (Figure 65). Black rolls a 4-1 and is momentarily safe: his 4 move is forced (B6-B2) and he removes the resulting blot to B5. White's prospects have apparently brightened, but a closer analysis shows he is still the underdog. Only eight rolls will force black to leave a blot. Equally pertinent, black cannot

FIGURE 64

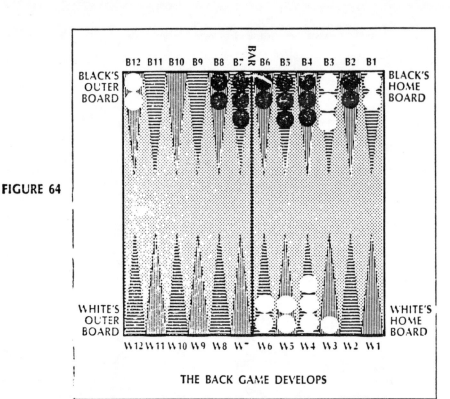

THE BACK GAME DEVELOPS

FIGURE 65

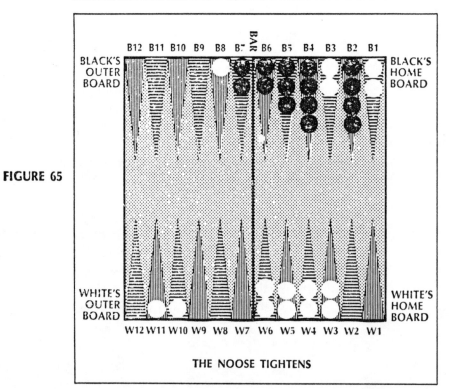

THE NOOSE TIGHTENS

make a move at all with four rolls and can move only half his roll with ten others—a total of fourteen rolls that slow black down just when white wants him to accelerate his progress.

A few turns later the position is shown by Figure 66. The dice have favored black. He has borne off twelve men without leaving a blot. White has run with one back man from B3 after all of black's men had passed him.

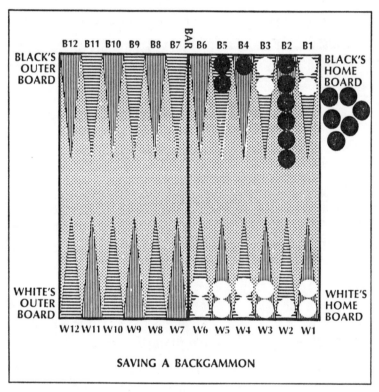

FIGURE 66

SAVING A BACKGAMMON

White rolls double 5s. What is your play? This is a tantalizing problem, so study the situation carefully before deciding.

The superficial winner is to use two 5s to cover the blot on W6 (B9-W6), constructing a closed board, and then to look for other opportunities. However, a closed board is small consolation after you are backgammoned, so your objectives should be (1) reduce the chance of a backgammon (you cannot avoid a backgammon unless you score a hit) while (2) maximizing your chances for a hit.

The solution is to bring out two men from black's home board (B3-B8, B1-B11). Probably the best move for the fourth 5 is (B9-W11), preparing to cover at W6 if given the chance. One man and only one must be left at B1.

Consider the potentialities from this position:

- Black rolls double 1s. Bad luck. He points on your blot and bears off one man. You now need a roll of 7 or better to escape a backgammon.
- Blacks roll any of the five remaining doubles. He bears off all his men and you lose a backgammon. Unavoidable.
- Black rolls two dissimilar numbers, excluding a 1. He bears off two men, leaving a blot on B2. You can hit with any roll of a 1, or, failing that, can get out to black's outer board to prevent the backgammon with any other roll except 3-2.
- Black rolls any 1 (except double 1s). He bears off one man and must hit with the other, leaving blots on B1 and B2. You are on the bar. Any roll of 1 or 2—twenty chances—will hit a blot. Any other roll gets you out of black's home court to save the backgammon.

Try this problem on some of your backgammon friends. Their answers will help you judge their skill level. Afterward, you can quote the odds in an offhand manner:

- 19.515% chance you will be backgammoned.
- 48.073% chance you will be merely gammoned.
- 32.407% chance of scoring a hit.
- Your chance of hitting and then winning? We would not hazard a figure.

Earlier (Figure 63) a position with white's pieces strewn around the table eventually developed into a sound back game.

Figure 62 illustrates the opposite condition—a well-developed position that shortly develops into a *nothing game:* by the time a shot opens up, white's pieces will be piled up on his 1, 2, and maybe 3 points, so that even if a black blot is hit he will have no trouble getting out and around the board.

Note the difference in white's position: the fifth man in black's home board is instead in white's home board, costing 18 spaces. White's three men in his outer board are worth about a roll and a half of surplus moves before his home board starts to fall apart.

Five turns later the position could well be this (Figure 67). White has run out of time and has been fortunate to salvage a 4-point board. Now he faces Hobson's Choice: a low roll

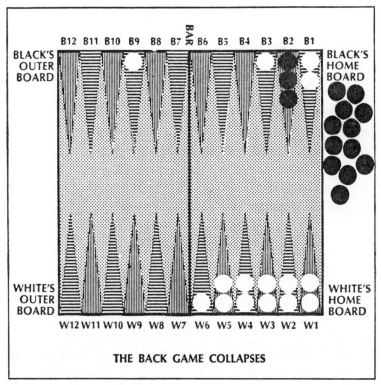

FIGURE 67

THE BACK GAME COLLAPSES

contracts his home board further; a roll of 4 or larger on a die forces the departure of a back man, ruining the back position. If this position could be duplicated in chess, white would gratefully resign. But here he must play on and suffer a probable gammon.

DARING TO HIT

In setting up a back game, you do not trouble to secure your men, but deliberately scatter blots around the table, hoping to be hit. Each such hit buys time, as it consumes at least half a roll just to come off the bar plus the rolls taken to return to the former position of the blot. In short, when you are far behind and choose a back game, resolve to get even further behind.

An experienced opponent will shun your blots when he sees you are preparing for a back game. Sometimes he will be forced to hit, as in coming off the bar on a forced play, or having no other play that avoids a hit somewhere on the board. Or the hit may be his lesser evil. Some fascinating positions develop during this jockeying stage: one player leaving enticing blots, the other agonizing whether to hit, eventually refusing. Then the tables may turn: the tempter's blots lead charmed lives until suddenly the tempter can score a devastating hit himself, abandoning the back game to go into a blocking game. The ramifications are, unfortunately, beyond the scope of this book. In fact, the back game deserves a book all to itself, with revised editions periodically, since expert players are still experimenting and developing new tactics in this area.

VARIATIONS ON THE BACK GAME

"Five men back" is the minimum for a playable back game, but more are welcome. Sometimes you can get six men back and even succeed in making three points. Then it is virtually impossible for black to surmount your barricade without leaving blots. Unfortunately, you are left with but nine men to start making your home board; stationing them strategically challenges all the ingenuity of an expert backgammon player.

TIMING, TEMPO, TACTICS

Chess and bridge players are familiar with the concept of *tempo*—or a unit of time. Generally the objective is to *gain a tempo,* to beat the opponent to the punch, to get one leg up in the race to reach one's objective. Sometimes, however, we want to speed up our opponent's play, for example, in bridge, forcing him to make a premature decision or to use up an entry he will need later. Or we may want to slow down our own play, conceding an inevitable losing trick early, so that a squeeze may develop.

Backgammon is truly the king of games with respect to tempo. When ahead, you rush forward to exploit your advantage in tempo. When you trail, you slow down the tempo, offering men for capture, waiting out your opponent, preparing a good board for the time a hit materializes.

The back game is but one manifestation of the importance of tempo in backgammon. Earlier we saw another in connection with the concept of contact: the player further ahead in the running count is usually obliged to run first with his trailers or back men, exposing them to a hit. In that connection, we also saw how keeping a man in one's outer board preserves a move of 6 on the dice so that the mid men need not be forced off their point prematurely.

Another device for slowing your pace is to create a position where you cannot move the larger numbers. In Figure 68 white rolls a 3-1 and seemingly has the perfect roll to make a five-point board (W5-W2, W4-W3). But how long can he hold it? Black will leave an immediate blot only if he rolls 6-5 or double 5s. In another turn or so, white will be compelled to move his interior men forward and soon will have a *nothing board.*

The farsighted move is to bring the men at W9 and W7 into the home board (W9-W6, W7-W6). Then you "waste" any sub-

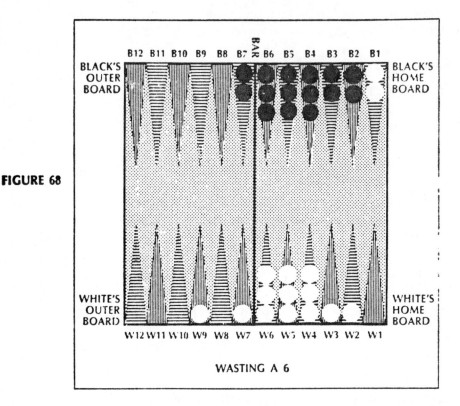

FIGURE 68

WASTING A 6

sequent roll of 6 on a die, for you cannot play it. The fewer moves you make in this situation, the better your chances. Time is not on your side, so you must find ways to conserve time.

The same principle holds with respect to a roll of 5. In Figure 69, white rolls a 3-1. Again the obvious move (W5-W1) is incorrect. White should vacate the 6 point (W6-W3, W6-W5), so that he cannot subsequently play a 5—or 6—roll. A few large rolls now will enable white to hold five points on his board, whereas he had virtually no chance of preserving a closed board.

Black can counter this ploy. Assume he, too, rolls 3-1. He can move forward from B6, B5, or B4 to keep white's men bottled up, but is that really his objective now? No longer. Black would be happy to see white roll a 6 and be forced to run one back man

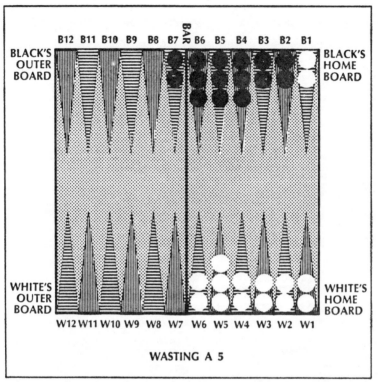

FIGURE 69

WASTING A 5

out, for then black can point on the blot with several rolls to wrap up the game. On all the other rolls black proceeds to bear off and grieves not if white's second back man runs as well. Black is 26 points ahead in the running count, about three rolls, a comfortable lead at this point.

Black's chief concern is leaving a blot that white can hit while white retains a good board. White wants to slow down to conserve his board and seeks a situation where he cannot move a 6 or 5. Black should not oblige, but should open up a playable 6 move for him. His correct move therefore is (B7-B4, B7-B6).

Everybody likes to win. The first few backgammon games you win will undoubtedly be running games where you get the lead and retain it. But real joy is the reward of a victory fashioned from alteration of the tempo—hastening your opponent's pace or retarding yours. The first such game you win will be a milestone in your backgammon career. Savor it well.

CHAPTER VI

Bearing Off

All the maneuvering and strategy in pointing, running, blocking, and tampering with the tempo are but a prelude to the decisive stage of the game—bearing off. For, in the final analysis, whoever bears off first wins.

AFTER CONTACT HAS BEEN BROKEN OFF

In a straight running game speed is the keynote. You have no control over the numbers fortune hands you on the dice (at least, we hope not), but you have the means to stretch these numbers to their greatest utility. Earlier one technique was shown:

- Try to advance a man to the next board with one die.
- And the corollary, try to avoid using your entire roll to send a man deep into the next board.

Even within this guideline you may have options. In Figure 70 you groan when you roll 2-1 and then settle down to find the best way to play it. You cannot advance a man to the next board, so how you move seems inconsequential. Not so. B9-B10, W11-W9 is the losing play; any other move improves your prospects. This is purely a matter of probabilities. With the first move, seventeen combinations of the dice on your next turn will ad-

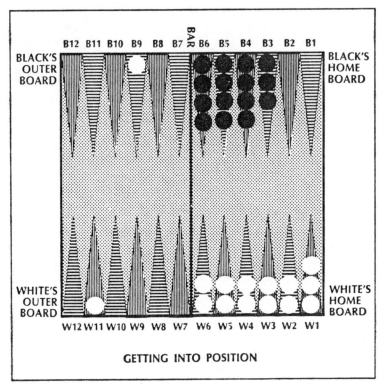

FIGURE 70

GETTING INTO POSITION

vance both men one board; with any other move, twenty-three rolls will do the trick. So give yourself the 17% break.

You are probably wondering how you can possibly figure this out in each situation, and is it worth the trouble. As to the latter, you will have to judge. But as to the former, the same odds apply here as in bearing off your two last men. The table on page 147 presents the exact figures, but there is no need to memorize the table, since you will shortly be given four simple rules that solve every dilemma.

For the moment, though, first calculate how far each man is from the nearest point in the next table: 4 spaces for the man at B9, 5 for W11, a total of 9. After you move your 2-1 roll, worth 3 pips, this total will be reduced by 3, to 6. So look up on the

CHANCES OF BEARING OFF THE LAST TWO MEN
ON ONE ROLL

Total running points	Position of men	Number of rolls that will bear them off in one roll	Favorable odds
12	6/6	4	11%
11	6/5	6	17%
10	6/4	8	22%
	5/5	6	17%
9	6/3	10	28%
	5/4	10	28%
8	6/2	13	36%
	5/3	14	39%
	4/4	11	31%
7	6/1	15	42%
	5/2	19	53%
	4/3	17	47%
6	6	27	75%
	5/1	23	64%
	4/2	23	64%
	3/3	17	47%
5	5	31	86%
	4/1	29	81%
	3/2	25	69%
4	4	34	94%
	3/1	34	94%
	2/2	26	72%
3 and below	2/1		
	1/1	36	100%
	2		
	1		

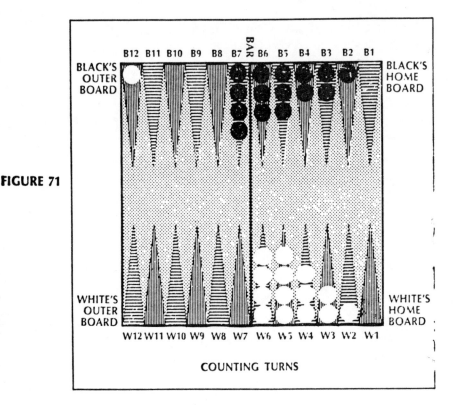

FIGURE 71

COUNTING TURNS

table on page 147 for 6 under Total running points and you will see that either 5/1 or 4/2 offers twenty-three possible favorable rolls, while 3/3 offers only seventeen.*

GETTING THE COUNT

By the way, how do you rate your prospects as white in this position? The running count again gives the clue. Your present count is 70, less the 3 count on the dice, for a net of 67. Black's count is 69, and he rolls next, so he has about a one roll advantage. Actually, he is further ahead, since he is ready to bear off and you are about two rolls away. But the margin should nar-

* One man 6 points from his destination is the best bet—twenty-seven successful combinations—but you cannot arrange that position.

row, for black cannot bear off a man on any roll of 1 or 2. Play it out on the board in back with random throws of the dice—recasting when a double is thrown, just to keep the match even. Black should win if he throws plenty of 6s and 5s and few 1s and 2s. Otherwise it should be a squeaker.

COUNTING TURNS

In Figure 71 it is white's roll. Who has the better chance of getting all his men into his home board and bearing off the first man?

You could use a variation of the running count to discover that black has 4 spaces to go for all his men to reach B6, while white has 7 before arriving at W6. Since it is white's turn, you might conclude he is about half a roll ahead.

Now try counting turns. If white rolls a 7 or better on his turn—twenty-three chances—he is home in one roll. Unless black rolls a double, he will need two rolls to bring home all four men at B7. Black's predicament is that two dissimilar dice cannot move four men.

Likewise, when bearing off, the number of men remaining loom in importance over the running count. Imagine that each player is down to two men: white has two men on W6; black, two on B1. Black boasts a 10-point edge in the running count, but that is scant solace for black if white now throws one of the four doubles that bear both men off.

In short, as the game nears the end, judge less by the running count, more by the number of men remaining in the crucial boards—the outer board when rushing for home, the home board when bearing off.

THE BALANCED BOARD

Much ado has been made of the virtue of a balanced board —men evenly spread out on every point. The advantage is incontestable: you are 98% sure to remove four men in your first two rolls. We question the unstated corollary, however: a board with most of the men stacked on the 4, 5, and 6 points is probably a result of mismanagement. On the contrary, an abundance of men on W5 and W6 indicates that you brought your men in economically. If you are behind in the running count, that dates back to earlier plays, poor dice, getting hit, whatever. But the lopsided pattern on your higher points is nothing to induce shame. On the contrary, feel proud.

We will put it in the form of a wager. Create any position you desire that meets these conditions:

- The running count is even.
- All our men are on the 5 and 6 points (4 also if you wish).
- Yours are spread evenly over the six points or even the first four or five points, if you prefer.
- To eliminate favoritism from the dice, we both move the same random rolls of the dice simultaneously.

We will wager that we will bear off first (draws do not count) and offer 6 to 5 (even money would be too greedy).

Here is one possible setup (Figure 72). Ready to play?

You say we pulled a fast one? Oh, because we have already borne off six men and your full complement is still on the board. Well, we have to have some men off to meet the conditions. Besides, what difference does that make, since the count is still the same. Why should it take you more time to roll 48 than us, since we are moving identical rolls simultaneously?

It will, not because we have fewer men, but because we will get optimum value from all rolls except possibly the last one or two. You will not. We will make almost every pip on the dice work for us, but you cannot.

We threw dice at random to demonstrate the economy of our position and the extravagance of yours (nothing personal). Of course, you can roll your own dice to test our thesis, but these were ours: 6-4, 4-1, 5-4, double 3s, 4-2, 5-3. Figures 73

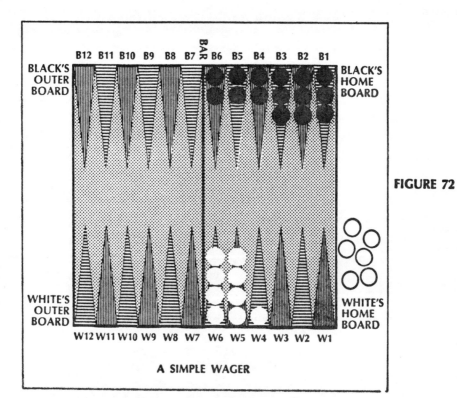

FIGURE 72

A SIMPLE WAGER

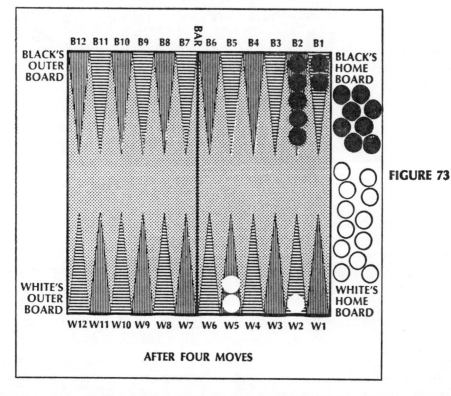

FIGURE 73

AFTER FOUR MOVES

and 74 show the positions after the fourth and sixth rolls respectively. Naturally black has narrowed the gap in number of men remaining, since he had the greater chance of removing two men per roll. The running count remains even; neither player has wasted a pip of the dice. But now comes a 4-2 roll on the fifth turn. White moves his two highest men down (W5-W1, W5-W3). Black bears off two men from B2, *but he has not received full value for the 4 roll.* A 2 could have borne off one of those men as easily, so black has wasted the difference, 2 pips on the dice. (If the roll had been 5-2, the waste would have been 3 pips; if 6-2, 4 pips, etc.) We are now 2 points ahead in the running count, since you wasted 2 pips, but we wasted none.

FIGURE 74

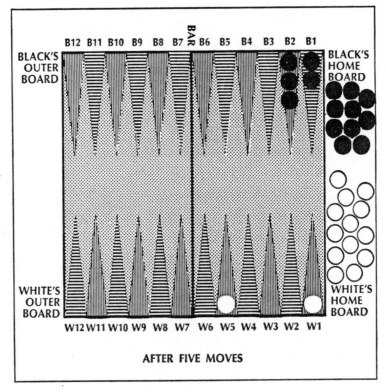

AFTER FIVE MOVES

The last roll does black in. The roll is worth 8 pips, but black can do no better than remove the two men from the 2 point. So this roll squanders 4 more pips, putting black 6 behind in the running count. White hardly notices, for he gets his last two men off on this roll and wins the game. Pay up! At that, white has frittered away 2 pips on the last roll.

To what conclusions does all this lead?

- Bring in your men into your home board as economically as you can.
- Don't waste a pip on a die to distribute your men evenly.
- Bearing off first is more critical to victory than is a symmetrical home board.

These caveats apply when you are in a true running game. While there is still contact, by all means cover your blots and make additional points in your home board, better to keep an opponent on the bar. At this stage, you should prefer making points from W6 downward. But do not delude yourself that it improves bearing off; every interior move cost you the equivalent distance a trailer could have traveled homeward, shortening the time before your first man is borne off. There is one set of rules for the contact game and another for the running game!

SHORTCUTS FOR BEARING OFF

Page 147 shows the exact chance of bearing off one or two men on the last roll. The precise number of chances in each case is not particularly useful, except when you are considering offering or accepting a double. Then you can pause and work out the chances on the spot. Remember, though, to allow for doubles: the largest four doubles will bear off two men, regardless of position. Double 2s bear off two men when the running count is 8 or more—except on W5/W3. Double 1s work any time the running count is 4 or less.

BACKGAMMON: THE QUICK COURSE TO WINNING PLAY

Working backward from the end position of the last roll on the table on page 147, we arrive at these commandments:

- Bear off as many men as you can on one roll in preference to making an interior move. Look up 4, 5, and 6 under the column Total Running Points and note that in the final position a single man has a better chance of getting off then two men.
- When you must make an interior move; follow these pointers *and in the sequence* given:

  1. Avoid doubling up. When you have but one point with two men, get the second man off there quickly. Whichever point has the most men is the one to be moved first. (Note in the table that two men doubled on the same point have the least chance of getting off in one roll.)
  2. Get off the 6 point. Otherwise in the two-man positions you will need a 6 (or a double) to get off—at best (W6/W1) a 42% chance.
  3. Bring your lower man down as far as possible (but not to W6/W1. Remember the preceding injunction about the 6 point; these pointers must be followed in sequence.) W4/W1 offers better chances than W3/W2; W5/W2 is superior to W4/W3, (however, W5/W1 and W4/W2 are equivalent).

OPPONENT IN YOUR HOME BOARD

Nothing is more disheartening in backgammon than the turnabout in the end game: you are bearing off; black has retained a point at W1; suddenly one unfortunate throw; you are forced to leave a blot; black hits and an apparent victory turns to a probable loss.

No position is impregnable. However, many of the turnabout disasters could have been circumvented. Therefore preventive medicine is in order. Our prescription calls for a mixture of forethought and safety:

- Anticipate double 6s and double 5s and take countermeasures. Even before all your men are home, position your men so that a large double will not cause a blot. In Figure 75 you roll a 6-3. Which man do you bring in? B11, for that leaves you safe even after a subsequent roll of double 6s and 5s. Play it out after moving from B10 first. A following roll of double 6s brings in the remaining man (B11-W2) on two rolls and you are forced to bear off two men from W6, leaving a blot there.

After all your men are home, try to avoid these dangerous positions:

- Obviously, any blot.
- Less obvious, a situation that can lead to two blots. In Figure 76 for example, either a 6-4 or 5-4 forces you to bear

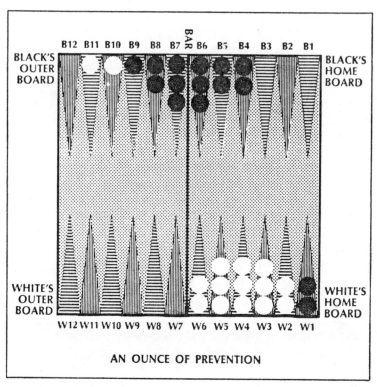

FIGURE 75

AN OUNCE OF PREVENTION

off one man from W5 and one from W4, leaving a blot on
each of these two points.

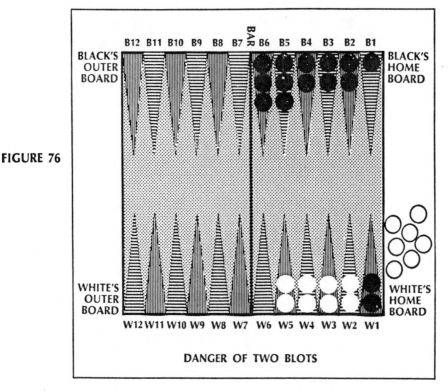

FIGURE 76

DANGER OF TWO BLOTS

- Three men on your highest point. In Figure 77 any 6 roll will
  cause you to leave a blot. This is an extreme position. If you
  had a third man on some of the lower points, the risk would
  be less. For example, if you rolled a 6-3 and had a third man
  on W3, you could bear off two men without leaving a blot;
  with a 6-1, you could bear off one man from W6 and move
  safely (W3-W2).
- Even two men on your highest point can be dangerous. For
  example, in Figure 78 there are twelve rolls that will leave

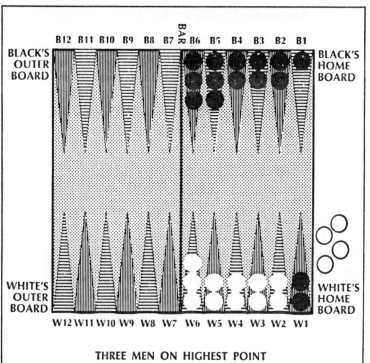

FIGURE 77

THREE MEN ON HIGHEST POINT

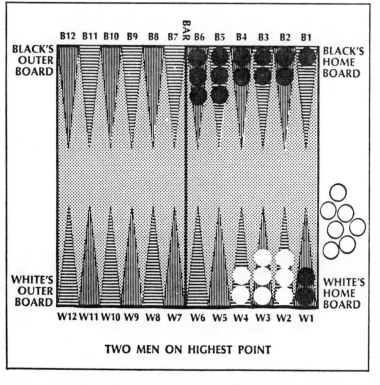

FIGURE 78

TWO MEN ON HIGHEST POINT

a blot: 6-3, 5-3, 4-3, 3-1, double 6s, 5s, 4s, 3s. Imagine that the two men on W4 were moved to W3. In that case, no roll would leave a blot.

- The fewer points you occupy and the more men on each, the safer your position, as the last example showed.
- Another position that is, oddly enough, quite safe is three men on each of your highest two points. No possible combination on the dice can force you to leave a blot. However, once you bear off a man from one of those two points after a roll or two, it becomes dangerous.

In contrast to the helter-skelter race when contact has been broken, safety is the byword when black holds W1. Nothing should please you more than to be rid of black's two back men, for by the time they depart you will have borne off several men and be far ahead in the game. Even the flight of one man is welcome, for that opens up the possibility of pointing on the resultant blot. Then black will come off the bar onto one of your higher points and you will be permanently safe from a hit.

Therefore, while you have the opportunity, use your small rolls to bring men off your higher points and pile them up on the lower points. At the same time, this acts as a stalling maneuver: eventually black will be forced to move within his own home board, and his strength there will gradually be dissipated.

Devote special attention to the men on your higher points, bearing them off or moving them downward. You try to maintain a solid phalanx in the process, for a gap of a single point opens up a greater likelihood that you will have to leave a blot. For example, in Figure 79 fourteen rolls immediately force a blot (6-5, 6-1, 5-4, 5-3, 5-2, 5-1, 4-1). Six others (4-1, 3-1, 2-1) are temporarily safe, but aggravate the position for the next roll. Say you roll 4-1; the only safe move is to bear off one man from W4 and move (W4-W3) with the 1. Now you have vacancies on both W5 and W4. On your next turn, you have only thirteen safe rolls (6-4, 6-3, 5-3, 4-3, 2-1, double 3s, 2s, 1s). What happened is that you can no longer use a 1 or 2 roll to move a man safely from W6.

Never underestimate the power of the point at W1. Its obvious function is to hit any blot that opens up, but its mere presence often forces you to leave the dreaded blot. You never have an option with a roll of a 6; you must bear off a man. However, rolling any of the other numbers will usually afford you the option of bearing off or making an interior move. Black's point at W1, however, precludes moving an interior 5 or a 4 from W5, or a 3 from W4, a 2 from W3, or a 1 from W2. As you continue bearing off, you face more chances of a bad roll. Moreover, as you empty the higher points, you have fewer options for each new roll. You have probably removed your third man from at least a couple of points, so have lost the flexibility of those surplus men. Two men on your highest point constitute

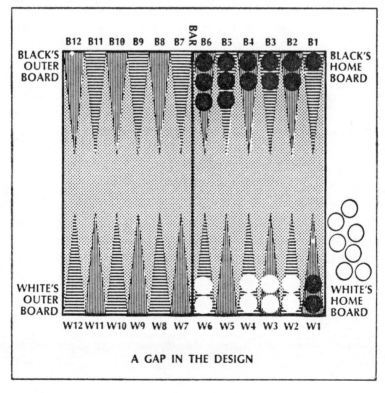

FIGURE 79

A GAP IN THE DESIGN

a particularly fragile position. Assume you have two men each on W4, W3, and W2. Any 6, 5, or 4, forces you to bear off a man from W4; only a 1 or a 2 on the other die permits you to make an interior move from W4. There are only eight dangerous rolls, but each of them opens up two blots. The disastrous rolls are 6-3, 5-3, 4-3, 3-2.

WHEN YOU HOLD THE 1 POINT

When the shoe is on the other foot, you tenaciously hold your point at B1 and frantically try to keep your board intact. Of course, you hope for an early shot, but if that does not materialize you eventually must ask yourself: "How long should I stay?"

There are two basic situations, each handled differently:

1. No reasonable chance to escape a gammon by running. (The gammon count discussed in the next chapter shows you how to estimate gammon chances.)
2. A reasonable chance to save the gammon.

In the first case, you stay almost to the bitter end:

- Maintain your point until black comes down to three or four men. Then run with one man, leaving the other at B1.
- When black comes down to two men, run with both men and at least save the backgammon.

Compare the situations in Figures 80 and 81. In both, white has run with one back man. In Figure 80 any roll except a double will give white a shot. Had he maintained a point on B1, black could play safely with any nondouble roll that includes a 1. In the current position, however, black must move the 1 to hit the blot, meanwhile leaving two blots himself. White has twenty combinations to make a hit in return. Even if he misses, the other sixteen rolls will get him out of black's home board and save the backgammon. If black rolls neither a double nor a 1, he will bear off two men. Then white has eleven chances for a hit.

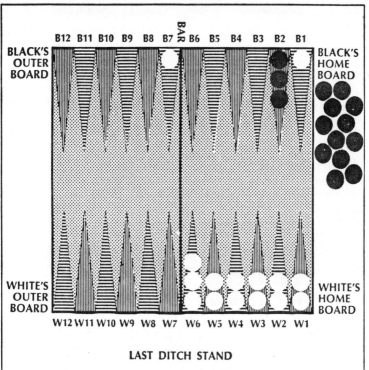

FIGURE 80

LAST DITCH STAND

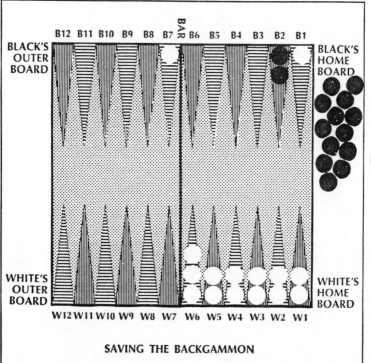

FIGURE 81

SAVING THE BACKGAMMON

Twenty-three of the remaining rolls get white out of black's home board to save the backgammon. The catastrophic roll is 3-2. It neither hits nor gets white past B6.

Toting up all the possibilities on our trusty pocket computer, we find that white's *expectancy* by leaving one man at B1 is −1.87, that is, he will lose 1.87 units per game over the long run with this strategy. If he ran with both men, conceding the gammon, his expectancy would be − 2. If you play backgammon only occasionally, it makes little difference what you do. But if the game gets in your blood and you play frequently, you will encounter this situation many times and .13 per game adds up.

In Figure 81, white should save the backgammon by running. If he stays, he must hope that black must leave a blot (any non-double roll that includes a 1, or 10/36) and that white will hit that blot (11/36 chance). The chances for both events occurring are just 8.5%, hardly enough to risk a backgammon. In fact, white's expectancy by staying back is −2.7, whereas by running his expectancy is precisely −2.0, the loss of a gammon, but no risk of a backgammon.

Now to the second basic situation, where you can save a gammon by running:

- Bring in your other stragglers first. There is no reason to rush the decision, since your back men may get an early shot.

- When all your stragglers are home and well deployed, reconsider the position. You might decide to tarry a turn or two, if there is still little risk of a gammon. However, unless black's board seems vulnerable, and you have surplus interior moves available in your home board, you better head for home and save the gammon. Even if you could be assured of a direct shot if you stayed and of a win if you hit, your expectancy is −1.08 by staying, and only −1.0 by running. This computation ignores the fact that you may not get a shot at all, or that you may hit and later lose the game, or that you could run well enough to catch up. These are three more good reasons to settle for a 1-unit loss.

The philosophical backgammon buff learns to accept and to minimize his loss, and to extract the most from the games where he leads.

CLOSED BOARD

If there is one ideal position in backgammon, it is to have a closed board with an opponent's man trapped on the bar. He must wait helplessly while you go about your business. However, as you gleefully bear off your men, you will have to open up points where he may be able to exit. So guard against leaving a blot, since a hit is about the only way you could lose the game.

Three general rules will protect you against almost all difficult rolls:

1. Avoid the danger position of three men on your highest point, unless accompanied by three men on the adjoining point.
2. Bear off—or make interior moves—from your 6 point first and then work downwards. This ensures that the man on the bar will not have a shot at you after he exits and also protects you against later complications.
3. Try not to leave any gaps as you bear off. For example, if you have one open point at W5, A 6-1 or 5-1 roll forces you to leave a blot.

CHAPTER VII
Doubling the Stake

Backgammon provides two ways of doubling the stakes: turning the doubling cube or winning a gammon.* Surprisingly often, you can combine both in the same game to win—or lose—four times the stake.

The gammon and the doubling cube are interrelated and together they present new paradoxes to bedevil the backgammon fan:

- A double proffered when you are far in the lead will not be accepted, and you will be the loser on balance.
- The apparent remedy of doubling on a slim lead often begets a disastrous redouble.
- In a straight running game, you should accept a double if the odds are less than 3 to 1 against you.
- Even though you are clearly behind in the game, you gain by accepting a double.

Backgammons are generally flukes—bad positions compounded by bad dice, or a double on the last roll not the result of design. Therefore, they rarely enter into one's conscious planning. Two nuggets of advice regarding backgammons: (1) offense—send as many enemy men to the bar as possible in the late game; (2) defense—get all your surplus men out of black's home board before he bears down to four men or less. Only two men are needed to secure a point; any more on that point are surplus.

- Although both players may concur in their evaluation of the position, it may be correct for one to double and the other to accept.

We will try to unravel these apparent inconsistencies, with a few side trips along the way.

First, don't wait for a huge lead before doubling, because then a gammon becomes a distinct possibility. Your opponent surely will not accept a double and risk a 4-unit loss (2 on the doubling cube times 2 for the gammon). When he declines, the game is over and you win but 1 unit. Had you been content to play on without doubling, you might well have won 2 units. Such restraint is unlikely to do you any damage. Should the gap narrow so that a gammon is improbable, you can later double to ensure your 1-unit profit. As a bonus, your opponent is more likely to accept then.

Second, doubling early on a slim lead is indeed poor tactics. Backgammon games commonly seesaw and you may then be faced with a reversal in fortunes and a prompt redouble. While most players offer or accept the first double on a rational basis, a redouble frequently induces psychological soul searching. The first doubler now wants to play out the game, hoping to regain the advantage and to vindicate his judgment in doubling in the first place. "But," he agonizes, "am I too far behind? I would not mind so much passing up a 1-unit game, but now the cube is already at 2. Maybe I should not have doubled in the first place —but no, I did have a good lead then. Is my opponent trying to pull a fast one on me? I would dearly like to play out the game and show him, but can I afford to with the cube at 4?" And so on.

A fresh attitude helps banish this needless mental torture: forget about the first double, pretend that your opponent is turning the cube to 2. View the position dispassionately and make your decision rationally. Whatever happened before is over and done with. You must play from the current position; regrets for "what might have been" will not help one iota.

Summing up, you should not double with a commanding

lead and jeopardize your chance for a gammon; nor should you make an early double with a slim lead, for the fortunes may quickly turn. Where does that leave you?

Doubling is the most difficult decision a backgammon player faces and the ability to make winning judgments on balance distinguishes the expert from the also-ran.

WHEN SHOULD YOU DOUBLE?

The problem breaks down into six areas: (1) the psychological factor, (2) the relative skill factor, (3) the positional factor, (4) the mathematical factor, (5) single-roll propositions, and (6) bearing off.

The psychological factor. In the final analysis, your double forces your opponent to pay for the privilege of continuing the game at a disadvantage. Poker offers the closest analogy: The player who feels he holds the better hand makes a bet, and his opponents must pay up in order to see his cards. Of course, in backgammon there are no concealed hands; all the action is in the open, but evaluations of the position may differ.

The doubling cube introduces other elements of poker psychology. You usually will have a definite preference whether you want your opponent to accept or decline your double, so a poker face is an asset. Reverse the roles and you may choose to play actor, deliberating a while before accepting a double that pleases you or quickly and cheerfully acquiescing on one that irks you.

The attitude of the doubler often affects the doublee. A confident double may cow the opponent into declining. A double by the stronger player may convince the weaker to surrender, mistakenly substituting the opponent's judgment for his own.

Every backgammon player has his own *doubling threshold* —the level beyond which he will decline all doubles. He may have a phobia about certain positions—two of his men on the bar, four men in his opponent's home board, two of his men back when his opponent has successfully run with his, four consecutive adverse points against him, or whatever. Perhaps he was burned in an earlier game when he accepted a double in his own particular nemesis situation. Regardless of the origin of his fear, he will be faithful to it, so you can safely exploit his bugaboo.

The doubling threshold of most players ignores the reality of the position. All they see is the dreaded situation recurring, so they quickly decline a double, even though by objective standards they may be far in the lead. Experienced players can steal many a game in this fashion. The true hustler cares little about winning the first few games—in fact, he is more likely to throw them as a lure—but he is busily drawing a profile of his opponent, setting him up for the later games when the stakes have mysteriously escalated "to liven things up a bit." He may decline a poor double from his pigeon to encourage similar doubles later, or offer a bad double and then play badly to be sure of losing the game. As he puts forth the image of a reckless, inconsistent player, he is intently sizing up his opponent, much as a boxer in the first round or two plans his knock-out strategy.

Doubling habits are observable in most players. Beginners tend to either extreme, accepting almost all doubles—since "they came to play"—or declining most, subordinating their judgment to their opponent's. Either way, they play into the hands of the shark, who adjusts his tactics accordingly.

Playing in his own league, the expert knows he should pull in his horns and double more cautiously, but his confidence in his ability and the urge to win the maximum overwhelm his good judgment. Against weaker opposition, the expert rightly doubles early, confident that his skill will equalize any lucky rolls his adversary may throw.

The beginner lacks the criteria to judge doubling situations. Not unnaturally, therefore, he holds off doubling until he has a commanding lead—just the time when a gammon is most likely. The hustler inwardly thanks his opponent for trading a probable 2-point game for a 1-pointer and then proceeds to go into his act, furrowing his brow, considering thoughtfully, and eventually declining the double with a reluctant sigh. The tyro cannot be blamed for thinking he has made a killing double and resolving to double again in like circumstances. When the roles are reversed, the novice cannot understand why the expert does not double with a collossal advantage. Later, when the hustler scores up a gammon, modestly murmuring something about lucky dice, his opponent is unlikely to connect the earlier decision against doubling with the final gammon.

Sometimes the hustler can have it both ways: in the process of discovering his opponent's doubling threshold, he doubles in a gammon situation and the double is accepted. The hustler purrs contentedly to himself, for he has just found a meal ticket. In effect, the price of a winning gammon has risen from 2 points to 4, while the cost of a losing gammon has declined from 2 points to 1, since presumably the naive opponent will double when the reverse position occurs. Of course, the hustler will find some excuse for declining regretfully. What could be sweeter than to have a 4-to-1 edge in the multiple-unit games?

We feel the psychological factor is the foremost in doubling decisions. For example, how else can you afford to double in an inferior position, except with the psychological awareness that your opponent believes otherwise and will decline the double.

Our one cardinal rule about doubling is: *double any time you feel your opponent will not accept,* excluding, of course, the cases when you have a reasonably good shot at a gammon. Every declined double nets you 1 unit. If you had to play out the game, you would need better than 3-to-1 odds in your favor to average 1 unit a game. Moreover, a double declined gives you 1 unit in less time, since the game ends abruptly with the refusal of the double. That leaves more time to play additional games, hopefully at a skill advantage, our next factor.

The relative skill factor. When the dice run even, superior skill wins. When the skill is even, the dice decide. Hence, the superior player can well afford to double more loosely than his weaker opponent. He is better equipped to strengthen his position, to extricate himself when things go badly, to play boldly to equalize the game, or to strike quickly to nail down a gammon. If his skill advantage also extends to doubling strategy, he is doubly blessed, for his opponent may decline a close double (psychological factor) or fail to discern the timely opportunity for a redouble.

The positional factor. The most mysterious factor of all. Oh, it is easy enough to construct clear-cut positions where every experienced player would decline a double. Figure 82 shows one.

FIGURE 82

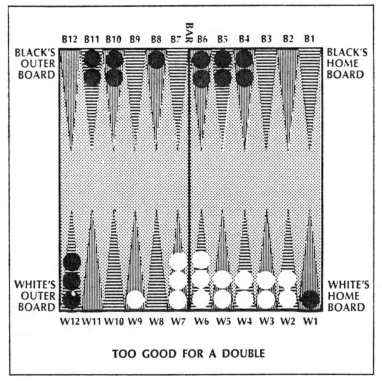

TOO GOOD FOR A DOUBLE

White will hit the blot at W1 and cover quickly for a closed board. Even if black scores an immediate return hit, white has the forces to keep hitting. Meanwhile, white's prime prevents black from escaping. In short, white is a favorite to win a gammon and for that reason he will not double in the first place. That is the trouble with all such strong positions: the likelihood of a gammon rightly restrains the player in the lead from turning the doubling cube.

Once the likely gammon situations are put aside, we are left with closer decisions and can only generalize on what constitutes a doubling advantage. Here is a checklist for starters:

- A good five-point board restraining a back man, opposite the opponent's three-point board or less.
- An opponent's man on the bar when you own the four highest points in your home board.
- Two of the opponent's men on the bar when you can effectively use one or two rolls of free play to consolidate or improve your position.
- Your opponent has set up a back game. Even though the outcome of the game is about a 50-50 propositions, you must double, since you stand to win 2 units for a gammon, but can only lose 1 unit.
- A clearly superior position when the running count is even.
- Equal positions when you have a significant advantage in the running count—in short, when you have a clear lead and a sounder position, so that you are a decided favorite to win. The further the game has progressed, the smaller the lead that justifies a double.

The mathematical factor. In a straight running game, the running count is your best measuring stick for doubling. Double any time you are at least one roll ahead—about 8 running points. Shade this to 4 or 5 running points when you have all your men in your home board, or a couple just outside. In this situation your opponent has fewer rolls left to get lucky.

If these margins seem narrow, remember they are under-stated by about 8 running points, since it will be your roll when you double.

Single-roll propositions. Every game has a crucial turn or two. Most players simply pray for a favorable roll; the expert gauges his chances before rolling and doubles if he has long odds in his favor. What exactly are "long odds?" you may reasonably in-quire. 2 to 1—twenty-four rolls out of thirty-six, shaded some-times down to twenty-two rolls. With probablities of this dimen-sion in his favor, the expert is happy to stake the outcome of the game on his one roll.

Figure 83 is a clear-cut example. White leads by 22 running points, but the position is so fluid that an earlier double would

FIGURE 83

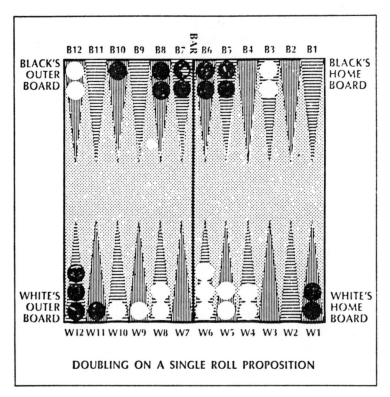

DOUBLING ON A SINGLE ROLL PROPOSITION

have been somewhat sporting. Now, however, white evaluates his advantage in terms of favorable versus unfavorable rolls. He concludes:

SINGLE– ROLL PROPOSITION

	Favorable rolls	Neutral rolls	Unfavorable rolls
Rolls that hit a blot (6-5, 6-2, 6-1, 5-2, 4-2, 3-2, 2-1, double 2s)	15		
Rolls that safely make the bar point (3-1, double 6s, 3s, 1s)	5		
Rolls that make W3 (6-3, 5-3, double 5s)	5		
Rolls that make W2 (6-4)	2		
Rolls that safely make W9 or W10 (5-4, 4-3, double 4s)	5		
Rolls that do none of the above, but leave no blot (5-1, 4-1)		4	
TOTALS	32	4	0

With this overwhelming edge white must double and black should decline.

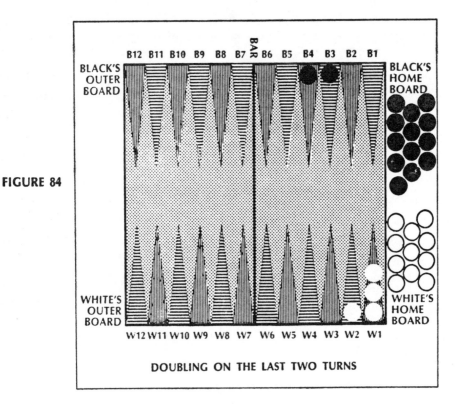

FIGURE 84

B12 B11 B10 B9 B8 B7 BAR B6 B5 B4 B3 B2 B1

BLACK'S OUTER BOARD

BLACK'S HOME BOARD

WHITE'S OUTER BOARD

WHITE'S HOME BOARD

W12 W11 W10 W9 W8 W7 W6 W5 W4 W3 W2 W1

DOUBLING ON THE LAST TWO TURNS

Bearing off. On the last turn or two the problem resolves itself into straight probabilities. Here is an extreme case (Figure 84). You are white and it is your roll. You should double even though you have four men to bear off and black has two. You are sure to get off in two rolls and a double would make you the winner immediately. Black must get off in one roll, if given the chance, and needs one of seventeen possible rolls—a 47% chance (actually his chances are less, since you may first roll any of five doubles to end the game immediately; actual odds therefore are 31/36 x 17/36 or 41%). On the last roll even a percentage point or two is sufficient to warrant a double.

Another situation: You have single men at W2 and W5, black has two men on B1. It is your roll. You have nineteen chances to get off in one roll—a 53% chance—while black is sure to get off if given the chance. Yet you should double. A vital factor in both cases is that you do not chance a redouble: if you fail to get off, no rule prevents your opponent from turning the cube, except that it is insulting on a sure thing that will obviously be declined.

Earlier in the end game you cannot estimate your chances so accurately. The best gauge is the number of turns required to bear off all your men. Figuring two men borne off for each roll of the dice, you decide you need eight rolls. Since you have but fifteen men, you can waste a half-roll—one number on a die. Still, you'd better figure on nine rolls to get off, allowing for the perversity of the dice.

What about doubles? you ask. Yes, double 6s are sure to bear off four men. As for the other doubles, you cannot bear off four men unless you have four men on the point corresponding to the number on the dice, or unless all higher points are vacant.

Sometimes, though, doubles bring catastrophe. In Figure 85 the one roll that will not bear off even a single man is double 4s. Oh, it improves your board considerably, but it costs you a tempo you can ill afford. Before your turn, both players were in a six-turn position—eleven men to get off. You have not improved your lot, but black is sure to bear off at least one man at his turn and will come down to a five-turn position.

Hence, we make no special allowance for doubles on the dice. We would rather be pleasantly surprised when we throw a useful double, meanwhile conservatively estimating nine rolls to remove our fifteen men.

To illustrate how half-rolls are wasted, let's take this same position two turns earlier. Then white had two men each on W1, W2, and W4. He proceeded to roll 4-1 and 4-2, bearing off both men from W4 and one each from W1 and W2. That vacated W4, so that any new 4 roll could not bear off a man. Similarly, after another 1 or 2 roll, the same number recurring cannot bear off another man.

An evenly distributed board is no insurance against wasted

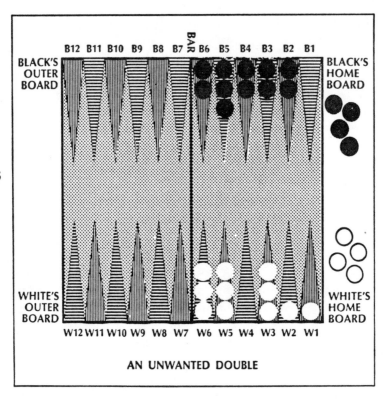

B12 B11 B10 B9 B8 B7 BAR B6 B5 B4 B3 B2 B1

BLACK'S OUTER BOARD

BLACK'S HOME BOARD

FIGURE 85

WHITE'S OUTER BOARD

WHITE'S HOME BOARD

W12 W11 W10 W9 W8 W7 W6 W5 W4 W3 W2 W1

AN UNWANTED DOUBLE

numbers on the dice. If you could only be sure that the numbers would turn up in reasonable rotation, there would be no problem. But frequently the same number comes up three times in short order—rarely 6s, or so it seems, but, diabolically, a number matching an unoccupied point or one sparsely populated.

Another oddity is that an odd number of men requires the same bearing-off turns as if you had one more man. You need four turns to bear off seven men—or eight. But in the former case you have a safety margin of half a roll—the number on one die—that you can waste without costing you an entire turn. We call it the *odd-man advantage;* it can be crucial in a close game.

Before offering or accepting a double in the end game, survey the position and make note of these factors:

- Number of men remaining and number of turns needed to bear them off.
- Odd number of men or even. With the former, you have a built-in safety factor of a number on a die that can be spared.
- Running points, now a rough gauge of whether you or your opponent needs unusually good dice.
- Position of the men: are they bunched up on the lower points, so that no rolls will be wasted? Are they evenly spread out or are there awkward vacant points?

All this sounds more difficult than it is. Usually a quick inspection tells you all you need to know. However, before you can give a practiced survey, you should examine the individual elements.

Now then, for some guidelines:

- In a full-board situation (neither player has borne off a man) double when (1) the count of the turns left is even, or favors you; (2) your opponent does not have the odd-man advantage; (3) you have a running count lead of at least 2 points; and (4) you have no more open intermediate points than your opponent.
- In a five-roll situation the same conditions apply except that you should double if you trail by no more than 2 running points. You can relax your standards, since your opponent has fewer rolls to get lucky.
- Take liberties also when you have the odd-man advantage.

When the game comes down to a three-roll situation you acquire a different kind of edge: black will not have a chance to redouble no matter how well he rolls. In Figure 86 the positions are identical, but it is your roll and therefore correct to double. Black should not accept, but let us assume he does. You roll 6-2 and bear off two men; he justifies his acceptance of the double by now throwing double 3s, cheerfully bearing off four men and regaining the lead.

At this stage, of course, black is itching to get his hands on the doubling cube, but must wait until his next turn. Meanwhile,

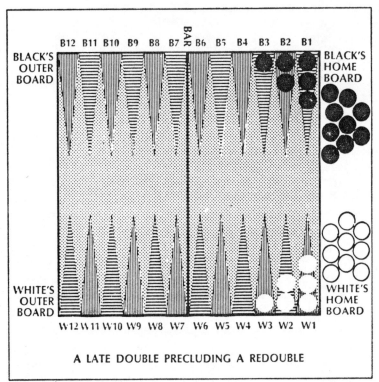

FIGURE 86

A LATE DOUBLE PRECLUDING A REDOUBLE

you have a chance to roll doubles yourself to pull the game out. But if you do not, you simply concede the game, as black is sure to remove his two men on his next turn. Thus you have had a free ride for your money: you have been able to play out the game without facing a redouble. Had the same situation occurred a turn or two earlier, black would have had time to redouble, and you would have been wise to decline. But by so doing, you would have lost the opportunity to throw the "equalizer."

THE DOUBLEE'S DILEMMA

Thus far we have dealt only with the decisions faced by the player leading in the game. Now let's turn to his opponent. When should he accept a double? When should he decline?

The following problem is a fitting introduction to this subject. White has single men on W2 and W5, black on B1 and B5.

Should either player double? If he does, should his opponent accept?

Answer: *Both* players should double, only black should accept.

Yes, this is a trick question: a player can double only at his turn, before he rolls. Whoever has the advantage of the roll in this position has a doubling advantage.

Let's work it out mathematically both ways. White's chance of getting off in one roll is 19/36, black's 23/36 (see table on page 147). If white rolls first, his chances of winning are increased by the cases when neither player bears off two men on his first turn; then white gets to roll again and is 99.7% sure of winning (the balance, 0.03%, allows for white throwing two successive rolls of 2-1). Thus white's total chances are 19/36 + (17/36 x 13/36), or 70%, ample to double with plenty in reserve.

Black, conversely, stands a 30% chance of winning, yet he should accept the double. To see why, assume ten games were played from this position. If black declined the double each time, he would lose 1 point per game, or a total of 10 points. Compare this with the outcome if he accepted the double every time. Now he loses seven games worth 2 points each for a total of 14 points, which is offset by the three games he wins, again at 2 points each, or 6 points. Fourteen less 6 equals an 8 point net loss. So by accepting the double black *loses less*—2 points less, to be precise. Put another way, black's *expectancy* per game is −0.8 by accepting the double, and −1 by refusing. All we have done is divide the total result by 10 to get an average for one game.

For black, a −0.8 expectancy is the best any ordinary mortal can achieve in this position. A clairvoyant could improve his chances, accepting the double only in the three games in ten he foresaw he would win, declining in the other seven. He would post 6 points for the winning game (3 games x 2 points) and lose 7 in the other games, for a net loss of 1 point or 0.1 per game.

Of course, it is ridiculous to figure odds for a clairvoyant. There is madness in that method. Yet, on reflection, is that not just the way many backgammon players reason? "This is the time I'll be lucky, so I'll accept the double," or "I don't feel lucky right now, so I'll decline."

Forget about the odds if you wish and rely on the feeling in your bones, or the glint of the bones in your dice cup. Your hunch may be right. However, for those of you who are not confident of your hunches, we suggest you resign yourself that you will probably lose a game in which you already trail. Accept the double, though, in a case such as this, where to reduce your *long-term* loss, even though this long-term strategy may increase your loss in that particularly game.

We recently doubled when our opponent needed double 6s, 5s, 4s, or 3s to pull the game out—4 chances in 36, or 11%. He accepted and promptly rolled double 4s. Were we wrong to double? Of course not. Was he correct to accept our double? Absolutely—in this one case. Nonetheless, we have readjusted our leisure-time schedule to accommodate this particular opponent for future games. In the long run—and we plan to play him for a very long run—his hunches may be less uncanny.

Now back to white's predicament in the previous position, if black offers a double. His chances change; he wins just 19% of the time—13/16 the cases where black, rolling first, does not get off, times 19/36, white's chances to remove his two men. Arbitrarily we will increase white's chances to 20%; it helps in the subsequent calculation.

Again, we project this position to ten games. If white declines every double, he loses 10 points; his expectancy is −1. Had he accepted every double, he would have lost eight games at 2 points each—a subtotal of −16 points—and regained 4 (two games worth 2 points each). His net loss, then, is −12; his expectancy, −1.2. Playing at a dollar a point, he has squandered

20¢; at $100 a point, he has given up $20.

Forecasting all this, white should decline black's double. From these two sides of the same problem, it is clear that somewhere between a 20% chance and a 30% chance is the break-even point for acceptance of a double. Actually, the break point lies midway between—25%.

This can be proved by playing just four games this time:

Declining each time—4 games times 1 point		−4 points
Accepting each time—		
loss of 3 games x 2 points	−6	
gain of 1 game x 2 points	+2	
Result of accepting the double		−4 points

This 25% figure is not some arcane secret, but rather one derived from a simple algebra formula:

Let X represent your chances, in decimal form. Then (1-X) stands for black's chances.

2X and 2 (1-X) represent the respective values of a doubled game. 1 is the value for an undoubled game.

$$2 (1-X) -2X= 1$$

or black's chances times a 2-unit game minus your chances, again times a 2-unit game, equals the loss of an undoubled game, or 1 unit. The equation solves to X = .25 or 25%.

When the odds against you are less than 75%-25%, or 3 to 1, or twenty-seven rolls to nine rolls, you should accept the double. When they are more, you decline. When the odds are exactly 75%-25%—assuming you can so determine—it is a tossup: follow your hunch or flip a coin.

HOW TO DETERMINE THE ODDS

That is the crucial question. On the last roll or two you can figure them precisely, but earlier positions puzzle not only beginners but experienced players as well. The better the player, the more reliable his "feel" of the situation. The novice needs specific pointers, so:

- When a gammon is likely, do not accept the double unless you have a least a 51% chance—taking into account black's chances on his next roll and yours on the turn following. Projecting beyond that is dangerous and difficult to figure. Again we arrive at the 50% figure algebraically:

$$4 (1 - X) - 2X = 1$$

When we lose, it is at 4 units—2 on the cube times 2 for the likely gammon. Working the equation out yields X = .5.

- When a gammon is not imminent, try to reduce the position to a one-roll proposition.
- Do not accept a double in these situations:

    1. You need to roll any double. Your chances are 1/6, or 17%.
    2. You need to throw a double, provided your opponent does not. In this case your odds are reduced to 14% (30/36 chance of your opponent missing times your 1/6 chance of succeeding).
    3. You need to make a hit and will have one combined shot. The best odds—when the blot is 7 or 8 points away—are 1/6, 17%.
    4. You have a man on the bar facing a closed board.

- Do accept the double if you need:

    1. A direct hit—minimum of eleven rolls or 11/36, 31%.
    2. One of two combined shots, totaling ten rolls or better—28% chance.
    3. A hit from a back-game position. When a blot opens up in black's home board, you will have two direct shots,

at least twenty rolls of the dice, a 56% chance. (Remember, 50% is the break-even point when a loss will cost you a gammon.)

Many positions are not susceptible to single-roll calculations and are therefore difficult to fathom. In these puzzling circumstances ask yourself these leading questions:

- Is it likely you will be hit and kept on the bar for a few turns? If so, you will fall far behind in the running count and may be gammoned.
- What are your chances of running when you have just one man in black's home board? When you cannot see daylight, decline the double, since after your blot is hit you will be nearing the gammon zone.
- With two blots in black's home board, can you reasonably expect to join them to make a point before you are hit? Once both men are secure you stand a good chance of getting at least one direct shot or two combined shots, sufficient to accept the double.
- When you have a point in black's home board—or are likely to make one—can you retain a decent board yourself until your opportunity to hit? If not, decline the double. What good is there in hitting when black can come off the bar easily and run home? By hitting you will gain time and narrow the gap, but it is foolish to accept a double hoping merely to lose the game by a narrower margin.
- A prime restraining your point in black's home board is not a sufficient reason to decline a double, provided you can hold your own board for a while.
- Assume your opponent will hit you at every opportunity when he holds a definitely stronger position—say, four points in his home board to your two. He should be going all out for a gammon, so allow for the possibility that your position may grow worse, even though at the moment there seems to be no shadow of a gammon.

REDOUBLING STRATEGY

At the beginning of each game the doubling cube rests in the center of the table. The moment the cube is turned, however, it relinquishes its neutral position and takes up residence at one side of the table or the other. There it is within easy reach of the player who last accepted the double. This means that he then controls the cube; only he can make the next redouble.

This simple rule leads to complex ramifications:

- Either player may turn the cube the first time.
- Neither can turn the cube twice in a game unless his opponent has, in the interval, doubled or redoubled.
- Until a player turns the cube, he has the inalienable right to double or redouble at his turn any time during the game.
- Once he turns the cube, however, he loses that right and cannot turn the cube again unless his opponent subsequently doubles or redoubles.
- In other words, once a player exercises the right to double, he loses that right.
- Hence the acceptance of a double bestows two benefits:

  1. The assurance that the doublee will not again be forced to choose between playing at twice the stake or forfeiting the game.
  2. The right to put exactly that choice to his opponent

Perhaps we have imparted too much mystery to the doubling cube, but only to stress the pervasive influence it exerts over the game. How different backgammon would be if one could double at will! Then a slight lead would lead to blackmail: the first double extracts a small price, a come-on, followed by more doubles demanding still higher prices. Under such rules the player who is behind could accept the first double only when he has good odds to better his position on the next roll. Playing on for the long pull would be folly, for the price escalates with each roll—and double—of his opponent. Under the accepted doubling rule, however, players enjoy limited liability.

REDOUBLING POINTERS

With this background, let's try to work out some specific guidelines for redoubling.

- Redouble anytime you are reasonably sure your opponent will not accept. This is the psychological factor again, and presumes you have no reasonable chance for a gammon.
- In all other cases, tighten up on your doubling standards. The fish is unlikely to get off the hook, and you will be glad you held back if he grows big enough to devour you. Say your opponent suddenly rolls well; if you refrained from redoubling prematurely, you can play out the game with the cube still at 2, rather than face the dilemma of playing at 8 units or conceding.
- In bearing off in equal positions, wait until you each have five turns before you redouble. That leaves your opponent with just two turns to throw doubles on the dice and still have time to hold you up with a redouble. (Remember, if you double or redouble in a three-turn situation, he has no chance to redouble following a good roll.)
- When you are ready to bear off—or when you have just one straggler in your outer board—redouble when you are two turns ahead—a lead of 7 or 8 running points plus your incoming roll.
- Earlier in the game, wait until you are two and a half turns ahead—11 or 12 running points—and have a superior position as well.

GAMMONS

The specter of a gammon lurks behind many doubling situations. The expert sizes up the chances coolly because he has been to that brink many times before. But the novice flounders in uncertainty, for he has neither the experience nor a measuring device to guide him. This section will provide the latter.

THE CRUCIAL POSITION

In one sense, the crucial position is the final one. Either black (we will assume black leads in all these examples) gets his last man off before you bear off one or he does not. A lucky roll or two by either player then or a turn or two earlier may decide the issue.

Obviously, though, there are grave risks in leaving matters to the last minute. The crucial position arrives when black is almost ready to bear off and you have men outside your home board. Examine Figure 87; it is fairly typical. Is there any way you can evaluate the chances of suffering a gammon?

FIGURE 87

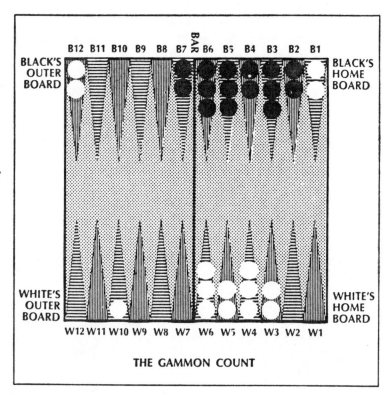

THE GAMMON COUNT

THE GAMMON COUNT

Here is a simple, fairly accurate means of judging these situations:

1. Count white's position (the player who trails) as follows:
   6 points for every man on the bar
   4 points for every man in black's home board
   2 points for every man in black's outer board
   1 point for every man in white's outer board
2. Add 1 point to your total to allow for the half-roll needed to bear one man off. The calculation can be done quickly:

$$2 \text{ men} \times 4 = 8$$
$$2 \text{ men} \times 2 = 4$$
$$1 \text{ man} \times 1 = 1$$
$$\text{and add 1 to bear off} = \underline{1}$$
$$14 \text{ total}$$

Each unit represents a half-roll—the count on one die—and the total gives a close approximation of the number of half-rolls before you will have borne off your first man. In this case, fourteen half-rolls or seven full rolls. This figure is meaningful only in comparison with black's count, which is figured as follows:

3. Count 1 point for each black man in his own home board. 2 points for each black man in his black's outer board. Once again, the total can be figured quickly in one's head:

$$13 \times 1 = 13$$
$$2 \times 2 = \underline{4}$$
$$17 \text{ total}$$

This total represents the number of half-turns before black will have borne off his last man.

4. Convert both totals to turns by dividing by 2. Remember

that an odd number converts to the higher number—
e.g., 9 units equals five turns. Thus white has seven turns
to avoid the gammon and black has nine to effect a gammon.

5. Compare the two totals:

- If they are even, whoever rolls next has the advantage.
- Otherwise, whoever has the lower total has the advantage.

In our example white should have little difficulty in escaping
a gammon. However, should he roll 2-1 a couple of times or black
come up with doubles on the dice, the prospects would change
quickly. All the gammon count can provide is an expectation
based on equal luck with the dice.

Let's try a few variations on the position in Figure 87 to examine how they would affect gammon prospects.

1. Two of white's home men are switched to B12, raising
   his count to 18, or nine turns. It is black's roll. A gammon
   is likely, particularly since black has the odd–man advantage, the luxury of being able to waste one number
   on a die.
2. Black has brought all his men in and borne off one. His
   gammon count is therefore 14, or seven rolls. Whoever
   rolls now has the advantage.
3. Same situation as 2, except that white's two men at B12
   now occupy W7, bringing his count down to 12. White
   has the safety margin if he rolls next, but only a slim advantage if it is black's turn.

The gammon count is equally useful later in the end game,
after black has borne off several men. In Figure 88 for example,
you, white roll double 6s. You can either run with your back
men or bring home two of your other men, hoping your back
men will have a later shot at a blot.

The gammon count gives the clue. This time, however,
project the position after each of your possible moves. First,
running with your back men to W12: that leaves you with a

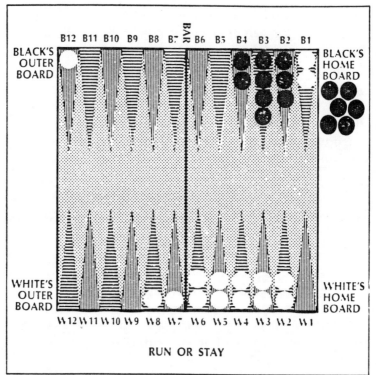

FIGURE 88

RUN OR STAY

gammon count of 7—2 for the man at B12, 4 for the four men in your outer board, 1 for the half-roll to bear off a man. Black's gammon count is 9—1 each for his nine men remaining in his home board. By running you have a good chance of escaping a gammon, since black needs five turns and you four. Barring disastrous dice, both players should get off within their quota, since both have an odd-man advantage.

Contrast with your prospects if you keep your back man at B1. All your other men will be home, so you will have a gammon count of 9, or five turns, exactly the same as black's. Since he rolls next, and the count is even, you are likely to be gammoned.

In this case, it is right to run. But if one of white's home men were moved to B11, that slight change would tilt the scales of the decision. Your gammon count after running would be 9, the same as black's. He has the advantage of the roll, so is a favorite for a gammon. Therefore, since you are unlikely to escape a gammon by running, you should stay back, hoping for a shot.

Earlier, we identified the crucial gammon position as when black is about to bear off. He will need eight turns to remove his fifteen men, on the average. Let us examine what positions for white are danger signs:

- Three men in black's home board. That alone adds up to 13 gammon points (remember the 1 for bearing off a man), with no allowance for stragglers not yet in your home board. If you wait a roll or two, black will have borne off a couple of men, coming down to a gammon count of 13 himself, and you will be in the danger zone. The solution is to run with one back man at the earliest opportunity. The third man on a point in black's home board is not needed there, but can cost you a gammon if left in place.
- Four men in black's home board. They count up to 17 points, more than black's total count as he starts to bear off. The only time you deliberately keep four men back is in a back game, when you occupy two points. The gammon count clearly identifies why an unsuccessful back game usually costs a gammon: maintaining your position intact keeps your count up to at least 17 points. Meanwhile, black is bearing off and lowering his count. So if a hit does not develop, there is no time to run for home.
- Two men in black's home board constitute a gammon danger only when you have a number of stragglers still to be brought home or after black has borne off about six men. The minimal gammon count for the two back men is 9, which is not, in itself, in the gammon danger zone.

The gammon count is equally serviceable for the player who leads in the game. As long as there is a good possibility for a gammon, he refrains from turning the doubling cube. When he senses a gammon is a possibility, he plays more boldly, hitting aggressively when he has the better home board. Prospects for a gammon egg on a good player and bring out his killer instinct. Few winning players settle peacefully for a 1-unit game when there is a chance for 2.

Oddly, the same aggressive style suits the player who trails. He takes desperate chances, hitting almost everything in sight to buy time or to narrow the gap. If he is lucky, he may equalize the position. If not, he may work himself into a good back game or a stronger back position for hitting a blot.

CAUTION: HANDLE WITH CARE

To our knowledge, the gammon count is original with us, and we have never seen it in print before. However, it is so simple and logical that experienced players may unconsciously use the same general approach, tailored to their own needs.

Like any general rule, this is an oversimplification that will work out well in the long run, but may be disappointing in a specific instance. For these reasons, we list below the bases for the rule and the exceptions that may occur.

- If back men are at B1, their starting position, the trip from there to W6 is 18 spaces, 2.2 rolls, or 4.4 gammon points. For ease of calculation, we have evened this off to 4. A conservative player may want to count back men on B1 at 4½ points.
- The value of 6 for a man on the bar is somewhat arbitrary. Obviously a half-roll is required to bring him off the bar, but who can tell how long it will be before a suitable number faces on the dice? We allowed another half-roll for this, figuring that even if just one point is open, the man on the bar has slightly better than a 50% chance of coming in on one roll.
- The men in black's outer board are presumed to be at B12, where white originally had five men and on which point

he would try to bring others to safety. On the average, one roll—2 gammon points—will advance a man from B12 to W6, a distance of 7 spaces. However, if white has men further back it is safer to count them at 2½ gammon points.

● The men in white's outer board are presumed to be at W9 or W10, where a roll of 3 or 4 will bring them home. If they are farther distant, it is safer to count them at 2 gammon points —one full roll.

● The presumption is made that once white brings in his last man, he can bear off with any number on the dice. Alas, this is not always so. Imagine your last straggler is at W12, W4 is vacant, and you roll a 6-4. You must use the 6 to bring in the straggler, but cannot bear off with the 4. Fortunately, this occurs rarely, so we have charitably ignored this painful possibility.

● Besides, it is offset by the rolls black misses. More often than not, he will require nine rolls, not eight, to bear off all his men. We have not built that extra roll into our rule, preferring to leave it as an unstated safety margin.

· ● White's last roll is in the lap of the gods and cannot be pre- dicted by any rule. One situation was just mentioned—the inability to bear a man off immediately after bringing the last man home. Another is that the last roll is just plain de- ficient—a 2-1 when you need a 4 to get in—or badly distri- buted—you have a man 4 spaces away but roll a 3-2, so both halves of the roll are consumed just in getting the man home, with nothing in reserve to bear off the first man.

● On a more cheerful note, you may throw more than your share of doubles and dispense with the gammon count. But so may black.

In short, we do not claim 100% accuracy for the gammon count, and will not refund the losses of those who lost a crucial point by following it religiously. Still, it is the best device we have found for quickly determining the gammon prospects.

CHAPTER VIII
Odds and Ends, Hits and Blots

THE MATHEMATICS OF BACKGAMMON

Backgammon can be approached without any reference to mathematical probabilities, but that would be a dishonest approach. Since the moves are determined by throws of the dice, which are in turn dictated by the laws of probability, some rudimentary knowledge of probability theory is needed.

Throughout this book we have alluded to percentages, number of rolls, expectations. Whenever possible we have culled the figures and offered general guidelines to the tactics favored by probabilities. However, you may encounter situations not included in any table that you may want to figure out yourself. Therefore, we offer this mathematical recap and rundown:

- The dice may be thrown in any of twenty-one combinations or thirty-six permutations. (A combination ignores the sequence; thus 6-2 is the same as 2-6; but these are considered two separate permutations.)

- Of these, fifteen combinations (thirty permutations) are nondoubles and the remaining six are doubles.
- A specific number can show up as a double in one way (out of thirty-six) or in ten ways (five combinations) with another number.
- To determine the chances of an event occuring in one of two ways, add the chances for each. For example, to determine your chance of hitting a blot with either a 1 or a 2, you figure the odds for each and add them together.
- However, be sure to exclude the overlapping cases. In counting the permutations for a 1 showing on the dice (eleven permutations), 2-1, 1-2, and double 1s were counted, so these three permutations must be deducted from the twelve theoretical permutations for a 2 showing on the dice.* Thus, the correct computation is $11 + 9 = 20$. Starting with the permutations showing a 2 instead, you would have $12 + 8 = 20$. The same result, but derived in a different fashion.
- A combination shot, requiring the correct total of both dice, is far less likely than a direct shot, where the right number on either die will suffice.
- The table of combination shots is unreliable if your opponent occupies any of the intervening points. Be sure to calculate your chances on the actual position.
- Combination shots do not figure in your chances of getting a man off the bar. If only the 3 point is open, a roll of 2-1 will not bring him in.
- To determine the chance of two successive events occurring when the second depends upon the first, multiply the probability of each. For example, assume black must roll a nondouble that includes a 1 to force him to leave a blot (probability of 10/36). Further, assume you must roll a 4 to hit the blot (15/36 probability). Then your total chances are $10/36 \times 15/36 = 150/1296$ or 11.57%.

* Including one combination shot, double 1s.

To determine the probability of an event occurring on any one of several rolls of the dice, you must resort to *negative probability*. Take the simple example of a 1 facing on either die when two dice are thrown together. It is simple enough to figure the odds of a 1 coming up if just one die is thrown: one chance out of six possibilities or 1/6. But you cannot multiply 1/6 by 1/6 to figure the odds of a 1 showing on either die. This calculation instead produces the odds of a 1 appearing on *both* dice: and indeed 1/6 x 1/6 equals 1/36, the probability of throwing double 1s. Nor can you add 1/6 to 1/6 and announce that the odds are 1/3. The fallacy of this approach becomes clear if you figure in like fashion the odds of throwing a 1 in six rolls of the dice: 1/6 + 1/6 + 1/6 + 1/6 + 1/6 + 1/6 = 1 or 100%. Yet it is possible to throw six dice without a 1 appearing.

The solution is to figure the odds of a non-1 showing on both dice. The odds of a non-1 showing on the first die are 5/6, and for the second die, also 5/6: 5/6 x 5/6 = 25/36, the odds of a non-1 appearing on both dice. Subtracting this from 1, or 36/36, leaves 11/36 odds for a 1 showing either on one or on both of the dice. Similarly, to find the chances of coming off the bar onto one open point in two rolls of the dice, the negative odds would be 5/6 x 5/6 x 5/6 x 5/6 = 625/1296, so the positive odds—the odds in your favor—are 671/1296, or 51.77%, better than an even chance!

This concept of negative probability, so helpful in figuring backgammon odds, is understood by very few players. If you can master it, you will at least be able to talk a better game than most opponents you are likely to encounter.

REASONABLE ODDS

The odds have been given for most situations you are likely to meet. And the preceding discussion should help in figuring out new cases that arise.

Here we are concerned with the reasonable odds you seek at various stages of the game. Most casual players are satisfied with anything over 50%. Yet everybody probably seeks at least 3 to 1 favorable odds in major life decisions. Sometimes even those odds are insufficient. Nobody of sane mind plays Russian roulette despite the 5-to-1 odds in his favor. Even if the revolver had 100 cylinders and still only one live bullet, there would be no sane takers. There is no gain in the gamble, and the loss is irreparable.

In short, odds are relative, measuring gain against loss. Translating this to backgammon, you should take reasonable and calculated risks after considering the gain sought and the loss suffered if unsuccessful.

An astute player willingly accepts odds of 70-to-30 against him when offered a double, for he knows he would lose more by declining the double. When faced by a likely gammon, he insists upon better than a 50-50 chance.

After accepting a double, one direct shot, an 11/36 chance, or 30.6%, justifies that acceptance. The opportunity of two separate direct shots or four favorable combination shots vindicates acceptance of a double in a gammon situation. In either case, the odds are 52%.

WHERE TO LEAVE THE BLOT

When a blot is inevitable, leave it where it will benefit you the most if it is not hit. In Figure 89 you roll a 6-2. You could run with a back man to B9, or bring in two mid men, leaving a blot on B12. But the standout move is (B12-W5), for if that blot at W5 is not hit, you have twenty-three ways to cover it for your fifth point toward a prime, and nine other ways to cover while giving up a point at either W8 or W9.

Early in the game you may sensibly decide to drop a blot on W5 or your bar point attempting to make your third point toward a prime. Black has better than a 40% chance of hitting, but this should not deter you. Again, the potential gain outweighs the

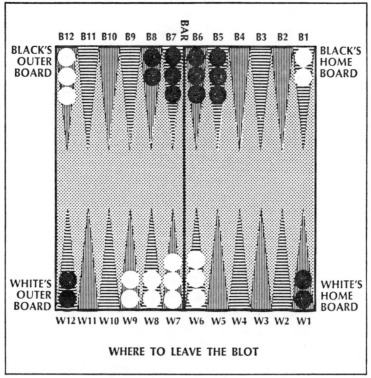

FIGURE 89

WHERE TO LEAVE THE BLOT

possible loss. If the blot is not hit, you have an excellent chance to cover and make a vital point. Should the blot be hit, the third man back is not that much of a liability.

The early game is precisely the time to go all out to build a good position, and this necessarily means taking chances. When you move two builders from B12 on a 4-3 roll, you are exposed to a total of eleven combination shots, equivalent to a direct shot. Yet you make that move willingly, not with trepidation, for it enhances your chances of making additional points.

The losses you suffer if hit are inconvenient perhaps, but not critical: half a roll to bring in your man off the bar, a tempo, 15 or 16 running points. This is a reasonable, calculated risk.

Later in the game, as black makes additional points in his

home board, you are not so certain of coming off the bar quickly. The table below gives the odds.

ODDS OF COMING OFF THE BAR

Number of open points	Odds of bringing one man off the bar in one roll		Odds of bringing two men off the bar in one roll	
5	35/36	97⁰₀	25/36	69⁰₀
4	32/36	89⁰₀	16/36	44⁰₀
3	27/36	75⁰₀	9/36	25⁰₀
2	20/36	56⁰₀	4/36	11⁰₀
1	11/36	31⁰₀	1/36	3⁰₀
0 (closed board)	0	0	0	0

Note, in particular, the difficulty of getting two men off the bar in one roll. These figures confirm the advisability of double hitting in almost all situations. By contrast, getting one off seems easy enough, but repeated trips to the bar will take their toll. For example, you have a 75% chance to get a man off the bar when black holds three interior points. In this situation, black will hit whenever possible; let's assume he hits you three times. You have less than an even chance in getting your man off on the first roll in all three cases! The probability for all three events occurring is 27/36 x 27/36 x 27/36, or 42%. Assume that you had two points in your interior board and you retaliated by hitting black three times. His chances of coming in every time on the first roll are 70% (32/36 x 32/36 x 32/36). Obviously, these are not the conditions under which you want to engage in a free-for-all of hitting and leaving blots.

The mathematical trap is to view each blot as a single incident. Sure, a blot open to a hit on 11 rolls is a good investment—69% odds in your favor—*provided that was the only blot you left during the game*. But you will have to leave others. If you leave two blots during the game, your opponent is a 52% favorite to hit one of them. Should you be forced to leave three blots, his odds go up to 67%.

Sounds frightening, doesn't it? The further the game progresses, the more blots you must leave, until finally the law of averages catches up with you. But not necessarily, for the early risks you take help you build additional points. Each such point provides a safe resting place for your incoming men. If you have built a sturdy foundation, you will need to leave fewer blots later in the game, when the stakes are higher.

In the later stages of the game, shots are harder to come by. A single hit then can decide the game, since a man on the bar probably must try to reenter a well-developed home board. Furthermore, the loss in the running count may not be easily made up, for the opponent may be so placed that he can be stingy about leaving blots of his own.

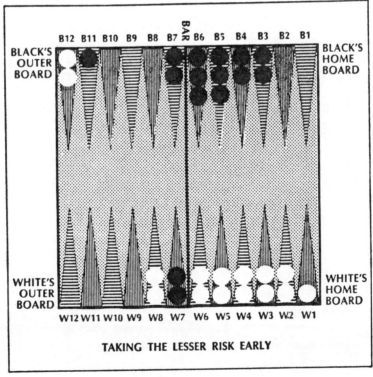

FIGURE 90

TAKING THE LESSER RISK EARLY

In Figure 90 white must run first, since he leads in the running count and the longer he waits the more his advantage will be reduced. He rolls 5-4 and has the choice of "playing safe" by moving two men off W8 or moving the men off B12, which leaves a blot. The general rule is to bring in the farther men first, since the nearer point is a point of safe refuge. And that rule applies here. Black will have eleven direct shots—a 31% chance—to hit the blot. While you should not be overjoyed with those prospects, you will do better by taking your chance now than by postponing your run for home.

The alternative, moving two men off W8, leaves you doubly vulnerable next time. Any nondouble roll that includes a 6 forces you to move off B12 and leaves black a direct shot 5 spaces away —fifteen possible rolls, a 42% chance.

There are many similar cases of taking the lesser risk early. Aside from surrendering the immediate probability advantage, the roll or two you tarry may enable your opponent to improve his board, so that if a man is sent to the bar, he will face longer odds trying to return.

THE LAST SHOT

As the last men race for home, there is considerable jockeying for position to determine who will get the last shot. In Figure 91 white rolls, trailing by 26 running points. If he rolls double 6s, he should bring his trailer at B7 all the way home; he must move him 6 spaces anyway, since he has only three other playable 6s, and it would be foolish to leave him at W12, open to a direct shot. Besides, with this fortuitous role, white has narrowed the gap to 2 running points, so might as well break off contact.

Double 5s are even better, permitting white to hit the blot (B7-W8) and make a prime.

A 6-4 also allows white to hit the blot and take over the lead. With the other thirty-two rolls, however, white's best chance is to stay back with his man on B7, out of range of a direct shot, and

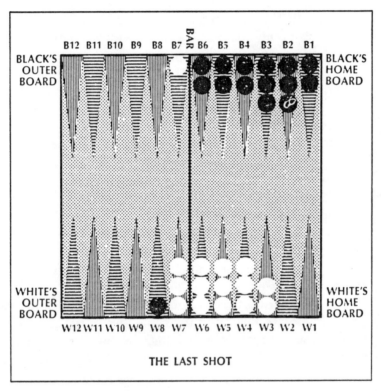

FIGURE 91

THE LAST SHOT

hope to get a direct shot at black's trailer as he comes around. Should white roll a 1 or 2, he should not inch forward from B7, but keep his ground, since each space white moves forward increases black's chances to hit or get past the blot.

Let's assume white rolls 5-2 and makes his 2 point (W7-W2, W4-W2). Now any roll of a 6 forces black to run with his trailer; in this event, he should use the entire roll for running, since once he is in range of a direct shot, the closer he nestles, the less chance of a hit (fifteen chances for a hit from 4 spaces away, versus eleven when 1 space away). Of course, if he rolls a total of 10 pips or better, he runs home safely.

What about the other rolls? Should black adopt white's tactic of keeping his man back waiting for a shot, or should he run with any roll? The waiting game poses perils, for white will be improving his home board as black is forced to break up his own. Moreover, white has two surplus moves available to play a 6, whereas black will have to run if he rolls a 6.

Our preference is to run with a total of 8 or more on the dice, which would give white a maximum chance of twelve direct shots at our man. We shouldn't have to wait long for a roll of 8 or better; the odds are 72% in our favor that we will hit the needed number in our next two rolls. (Seventeen rolls of the dice total 8 or better, so the negative odds are 19/36 x 19/36, which equals 28%; the positive odds are therefore 72%.)

What are our chances if we wait for a total of 10 or better on the dice? Only eight rolls total 10 or better. We have to wait three rolls to have just a 53% chance of coming up with a 10 or better. That is playing it a bit close, particularly since we cannot wait out the dice if we roll, say, 6-1.

The general rule, therefore, is to stay back, beyond direct shot range, if you are behind in the game, but to run, choosing the best time and a reasonable number on the dice, when you are leading.

CLOSE DECISIONS

Experts play rapidly, for there are few situations they have not encountered before. Yet they will pause at times to work out the move offering the best mathematical chance. For an expert to leave a blot subject to twelve shots when he could have left one open to only eleven is a grievous error in his way of thinking. To the casual player the difference of 1/36, or 2.8%, is miniscule, but the expert cannot afford these bad habits, for the 1/36 edge mounts up over the thousands of games he plays each year.

Our advice to the occasional player is to concentrate more on general tactics: when to run, hit, temporize, maintain contact, break contact. Do not agonize over the exact odds in each situation, for backgammon will then become a colossal bore. Perhaps once or twice during a game you should pause to puzzle out a crucial move; for the rest, you will do well enough—and enjoy yourself more—if you are on the right side of the 70-30 propositions. If you must err, let it be on those "close decisions" where there is a 2% edge either way. You can afford to go astray there and conserve your mental energy for more important matters.

As a curiosity, we present the following "close decision." It is white's turn and he has one man on W3, three men on W1. Black has one man on B6, another on B3. White doubles. Should black accept?

Do not bother to figure it out. Remember, this is just a curiosity. Besides, it took us twenty minutes with a pocket calculator, supplemented by tables of statistics compiled earlier. Our point is that nobody could possibly work out the figures at the table.

Superficially, black should decline the double, since his chances of winning are 24.69%, a shade less than the 25% break-even point. White wins immediately if he rolls any of the four highest doubles; if not, black has ten possible rolls on the dice that will get him off in one roll; otherwise white will win on his second roll.

So the apparent calculation is: 32/36, the cases where white does not get off on his first roll, times 10/36, black's chance of getting off in one roll = .2469, black's chances to win.

Ah, but this overlooks the possibility that white may roll 2-1, bearing off but one man. Black would then become an 85% favorite and would redouble, and white should decline.

So black's true chances are $(30/36 \times 10/36) + 2/36 = 28.7\%$, sufficient for black to accept white's initial double. The extra 2/36, or 5.55%, chance of white's throwing 2-1 tip the scales. Thus what looks like a "close decision" for declining the double becomes a "close decision" for accepting.

So what! Nobody could figure out the odds at the table anyway; even if they could, who cares? Only an author who is trying to give a complete survey of this fascinating game and to warn his readers away from esoterica. And possibly the professional who plays perhaps 10,000 games a year, on which his livelihood depends.

HOW TO SPOT A HUSTLER

As in any game of skill, the best way to improve is to play against, or take lessons from, a professional. Unfortunately, the top players are not particularly interested in giving lessons. They can spend their time more profitably playing at $100 a point and upward. You are unlikely to get into that kind of game—for long—with the very top players.

At the next level, though, you are likely to encounter the hustler who makes his living from backgammon less obviously. Nothing in his appearance is likely to give him away, for until recently backgammon was purely an upper-crust game, where he probably learned his craft. A Dun and Bradstreet rating might be a more accurate tipoff, but not entirely reliable, since some wealthy scions of noble houses can truly be termed hustlers. They do not need the income, but since they are fascinated by backgammon, they are willing to reap the rewards.

A hustler, then, we define as anyone who plays a top game of backgammon, conceals that fact, and seeks to make money from less gifted players. You may decide to play against one in an effort to learn more about the game. In that case, be prepared to pay top dollar for the education.

Being hustled once is no tragedy. The real losers are those who keep coming back for more in unequal contests. Better to get burned once early. Horse racing comes to mind. We must confess to a certain knack for betting the horses. Years ago we spent our first evening at the track, bet eight races, and lost eight. You may wonder what could be worse luck. Well, we could have won all eight races. Then we might think we had some special talent and still be trying to exploit it.

Anyone with a significant skill advantage possesses the first attribute of the hustler. In the 40s we tried out for a college chess team, playing two trial games against the would-be captain. We pushed him all over the board, but made two trivial errors that diabolically cost us both games. Not until the following week did we learn that we had been over-matched against the fifteenth-ranking American chess master, who was giving us room to show our skill. He had the natural equipment to be a hustler but too much pride to lose a game deliberately.

Pride goeth before a money game. So, assuming that most newcomers to backgammon do not relish the idea of being hustled, we shall offer some tips for identifying this breed. In Chapter VII, while discussing the doubling cube, we pointed out that the hustler tries to establish his opponent's doubling threshold, deliberately doubles, or accepts doubles in odd circumstances to establish an image of irresponsibility and to set up his pigeon for the kill. Here are some other characteristics of the hustler.

- He starts out losing, but ends up winning. The early games are mere exercises to whet the avarice of the pigeon and convince him that he is indeed the superior player.
- Somehow the stakes are increased toward the end. Even afterward, the innocent loser may wonder how the price escalated. Rarely will he be conscious of pressure from his accommodating opponent. Rather, it seems that both players had mutually decided to up the ante for the last few games to add more excitement. By a strange coincidence, the hustler won every one of those crucial games.
- All kinds of interesting innovations creep into the game. The common characteristic is that they increase the stakes. The hustler believes in *automatic doubles,* that is, when the first roll is a double, the doubling cube is automatically turned once; a second double automatically gives it another turn. Another favorite of the hustler is the *optional reroll:* if the first player does not like his roll, he can reroll, but only after turning the doubling cube once. Usually in this variation, the second player is extended the same courtesy. A third

device is known as the *beaver,* whereby the player doubled has the option of turning the cube once more and keeping it on his side of the table. Parenthetically, we should add that many nonhustlers are addicted to these innovations simply because they add zest to the game. So do not conclude that a player is a hustler because he seeks wide-open gambling gimmicks.

- The hustler plays rapidly and effortlessly, almost as if he does not care. Part of this is an act to put his opponent off guard, part a mark of his confidence, and part because he can immediately choose the best move from his vast experience.

- The hustler does not give lessons. He sees no reason to improve the game of his meal ticket. Moreover, he wants to convey the image of a lucky, impulsive player, not a shrewd, calculating gambler. So he will not offer advice and will answer vaguely if you solicit it.

- The hustler seems to get more lucky rolls than the next fellow. This is because he has maneuvered himself into flexible positions where few combinations on the dice can hurt him. When a good one turns up, it is more a matter of favorable probabilities than blind luck.

- The hustler is inclined to early doubles on a slim lead. When his opponent refuses, he gains a sure 1-unit profit in a minimum of playing time. When the double is accepted, the hustler's skill advantage should see him through. If not, his opponent is unlikely to diagnose the right time to redouble.

- The hustler misreads his dice more than most players. Everybody occasionally errs in this department, but the hustler more than most. Naturally his actual move is more to his advantage than the numbers on the dice. Usually he gets away with the deception, because most players concentrate on their own plays and virtually ignore their opponents'. Should you catch the hustler moving incorrectly and draw it to his attention, he will apologize profusely and probably abandon the practice. From his vantage point, the extra edge is useful, but not vital.

● The hustler occasionally makes the oddest moves—a dangerous hit, a timid reluctance to hit, dropping an unnecessary blot. Sometimes he is acting the part of a foolish, reckless player as part of his con game. More often, he has decided to act boldly in a desperate situation or to play safe in a comfortable one. But his considered expert judgment may not agree with yours, so his move may strike you as bizarre.

Backgammon is the hustler's paradise. Not only is it the finest gambling game devised by man, but it also defies precise analysis. Paradoxically, even after a game has been completed, the players cannot be sure whether either made the right move at a crucial time, but only how the chosen move turned out. Thus it is that the weakest novice can win a crucial game against the greatest expert.

The sure protection against the hustler is to start at a low stake and refuse to raise it, shunning also automatic doubles, optional rerolls, beavers, and any other enticing "multiplier" your opponent may suggest. If he is indeed a hustler and continues to play with you, he must enjoy your company.

CHOUETTE

Chouette is an exciting variation of backgammon in which three or more players can participate. One man, known as the *man in the box,* or the *box,* plays against the others and his stakes are increased proportionately to the number of opponents he faces. If he is arrayed against three players, the box plays at triple the agreed stake to match the total commitment of his opponents, each playing at the regular stake.

Each player rolls a die and the one with the highest number becomes the box; the next highest is designated *captain,* the player who actually plays against the box. All the others become teammates of the captain. The numbers on their dice determine the sequence by which they later ascend to captain and then to the man in the box. The captain rolls the dice and makes the moves, but in consultation with his teammates. They can make no move on their own, other than to decline a double or redouble offered by the box. In this case, the decliner loses the number of units on the cube before it was turned.

After each game the loser goes to the bottom of the ladder of the captain's team. The winner retains his seat and plays again. If the box loses, the captain takes over his position and all the captain's teammates move up one notch each, so that the senior teammate becomes captain.

These are the basic rules for chouette, but there are many variations and opportunities for settlements. We mention the game briefly for two reasons: first, since the players consult, you can learn a good deal about the various playing and doubling styles by watching a chouette or playing in one—but only on the captain's team! (Everybody seeks to become the box so he can play at the larger stake, so nobody will object if you decline that honor, particularly if you agree to go to the bottom of the ladder.) Secondly, doubles and redoubles abound in chouette, partly as a means of putting the box under pressure, partly for the sheer excitement that becomes contagious. Therefore, try to play at a lower stake than in a two-handed game, and be sure to decline your chance at the box until you know a great deal more about the game.

Oh, yes, hustlers play chouette too.

TO HIT OR NOT TO HIT

After the first few moves a backgammon game fairly bristles with decisions. The basic ones, listed in descending order of difficulty are:

- To accept a double
- To offer a double
- To hit or not
- To run or stay

All but the third have been thoroughly explored. We have left hitting for last for good reason: hitting decisions occur all throughout the game until contact is broken. The winner is not necessarily the one who hits firstest and mostest. After all, the objective is rather to bear off all of one's men ahead of the opponent's.

Still, it is correct to hit in most cases. These are two more situations where a hit is indicated:

To avoid a double. In Figure 92 unless you take drastic action, black will double at his next turn. Thirty-two rolls will enable black to construct a fifth point toward his prime or to bring his back man safely past your mid men. Moreover, he already has a

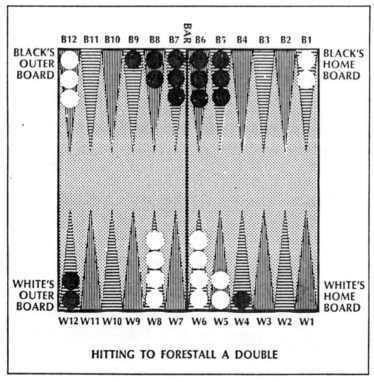

FIGURE 92

HITTING TO FORESTALL A DOUBLE

better position and leads by 27 running points. Hence the double is a stand-out proposition for black.

Of course, if you roll 4-2, double 4s, 2s, or 1s, you can point on his blot and black may be dissuaded from turning the cube. But let's assume you fail to get a perfect roll and instead turn up some combination of 2, 4, or 9. If you make a neutral move, black will double and you should probably refuse. You are not far enough behind in the running count to maintain a good board while waiting for a shot that may never develop.

How about hitting black's blot instead? That puts a blot of your own on W4. Black may double anyway, but now you can accept. If black hits your blot, you will not mind a third man back, for that slows down your game so that you have a reasonable chance to hold a good home board in hopes of a shot. If he fails to hit, you hope to cover quickly at W4 and perhaps hit again.

Equally important, hitting deprives black of the opportunity to point on B4 with twelve rolls that would otherwise accomplish that objective—any combination of 5, 3, 2, and 1—since he must use the number on one die to bring his man in. Our recommended action—indeed a desperate move—may not stave off the double, may not save you the game, and may actually induce you to accept a double and later lose the game. But it is your best option under the circumstances.

This kind of reasoning also clears one's head, so that if you roll something horrendous, such as 6-5, you can cheerfully decline black's double. Not that you should puzzle out all the possibilities before each roll; that is as much a waste of mental effort as deciding how to play a bridge hand after a different opening lead. No, see what comes upon the dice and then plan your strategy. The only exceptions to this are when you are contemplating a double or your opponent has just turned the cube.

A second reason for hitting is:

To improve your chances for a gammon. Figure 93 illustrates a typical situation. White leads by 45 running points, or almost

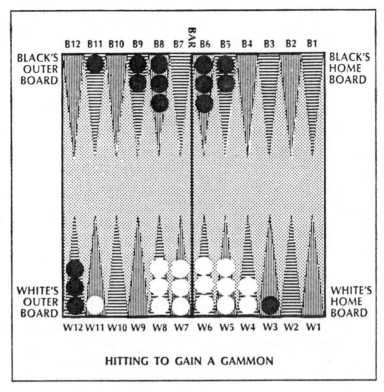

BLACK'S OUTER BOARD

BLACK'S HOME BOARD

B12 B11 B10 B9 B8 B7 BAR B6 B5 B4 B3 B2 B1

WHITE'S OUTER BOARD

WHITE'S HOME BOARD

W12 W11 W10 W9 W8 W7 W6 W5 W4 W3 W2 W1

FIGURE 93

HITTING TO GAIN A GAMMON

six rolls, not yet a good run at a gammon. Figuring gammon points, white has 22, while black has 17, so white has work to do to get into gammon range.

White rolls 6-5. He could play safely (W11-W6, W8-W2), but if black rolls a 6 himself, he will run his back man and the gammon chance will vanish. White should then double, and black would decline.

To keep gammon chances alive white should hit the blot (W8-W3x). If black cannot come off the bar immediately, or misses your blot on W3, you have good prospects of covering, hitting again, pointing on the blot, and otherwise harassing black's back man. Eventually, you may be able to hit the blot and produce a closed board. Meanwhile, each time black comes off the bar, he has only half a roll to advance his other men. Let's assume that black gets three men in from his outer board and then is frozen out after you hit the blot and make a closed board. Black's gammon count would be 16 and you become a favorite to score a gammon.

On the other hand, if black hits white's blot, you are still far enough ahead to double, and black would probably decline. In short, the hit has a gammon to gain and nothing to lose.

WHEN NOT TO HIT

There are so many situations where a hit is indicated that a listing of situations where you should *not* hit may be instructive:

- You have an outstanding alternative play. For example, black drops a blot at B5 on his first turn, and you roll double 1s. To waste the entire roll to hit would be short-sighted, since you could instead make two valuable points at W7 and W5.
- You are sure of a gammon, or a regular game that offers no gammon chances. Hitting lets your opponent back into your home board, where he may score a lucky hit and turn sure victory into a possible loss. Obviously unsound.
- Your opponent is setting up a back game. If he already has four men back, do not help him get the vital fifth man into position—or a sixth man, for that matter. He desperately needs to slow down the pace; do not help him.
- You must leave a blot of your own in your home board. Sometimes this is worthwhile, as when you are battling for your 5 point, or in the two situations just given—when you are trying to stave off a double or nail down a gammon. Otherwise, it rarely pays to hit and leave a blot on W1 or W2, or even W3, unless you have made the adjoining higher points.
- You are waiting for a shot but it develops prematurely, before your home board is set up. You would short-change yourself by hitting, since black should have no difficulty in getting off the bar and running home. And what have you accom-

plished? Breaking up your valuable point on black's side of the table, slowing down his pace just when you want to accelerate it, wrecking your timing and strategy.

- When your home board has a blot or two of its own or when you are open to an uncomfortable number of return shots yourself. Nobody is likely to hit in this case, but we include it here anyway, just for the sake of completeness.

One last word of caution: a single hit sometimes leads to a wild blot-hitting slugfest. Do not get yourself into this kind of free-for-all when your opponent has more points in his home board than you. He will be delighted to slug it out with you, because each such exchange gives him better odds.

TOURNAMENT PLAY

Backgammon tournaments are becoming increasingly popular. We heartily recommend entering them, starting with the beginner events.

Three types of tournament are generally run:

Elimination events. This is the choice in the prestigious tournaments where leading players compete. The winner of each match progresses to the next until finally the two undefeated players meet in the finals. Those who lose in the first, or perhaps the second, round go into a consolation flight. Tennis players are familiar with this arrangement. Matches are for a specified number of points—5, 7, 9, or as many as 21, but always an odd number. The first player to reach the required total wins. Usually there is no limit on doubles, but automatic doubles are barred.

Round-robin events. There is no elimination. Instead, the players are divided into two groups. The players in one group play short matches—generally two or three games—against as many players in the other group as time allows. Automatic doubles are barred, and a maximum of one double and one redouble is permitted.

Duplicate events. A novel variation, taken from bridge tournaments, which can be applied to either of the above. The director throws the dice for all the players. Theoretically, all games should develop along similar lines, but actually the variations are so great that no one would guess they proceeded from identical rolls.

A fourth possibility, which we predict will become increasingly popular, is a Swiss tournament, which combines the best elements of the elimination and round-robin movements. This term, too, is borrowed from the bridge world. Short matches are played, as in a round-robin tournament, but then the winners are paired against winners and the losers against losers. Seeking the most equal match-ups, the director sorts out the score slips and pairs the two players with the closest scores. New pairings are arranged after each round according to the net cumulative scores of the players. Sometimes the director must juggle the pairings to avoid two players from competing against each other a second time.

Among the advantages of a Swiss tournament are: (1) when the field is uneven, most of the players will be competing at their own level after a round or two; and thus, (2) everybody gets a reasonable chance to win a match or two; (3) the eventual winner is usually decided on the last round in a head-to-match between the two leaders; this overcomes the frustration of finishing in the runner-up position, never having played against the eventual winner (whom you certainly would have vanquished); (4) the suspense and excitement mount with each round, for a player can lose a couple of matches by slim margins and then suddenly emerge into the big league with one convincing victory; (5) in effect, the tournament consists of several smaller ones at different levels which constantly change with the results of each round.

One warning before you organize a Swiss tournament: this type of event requires the services of a facile and experienced director, for otherwise there may be interminable waiting around between rounds as he sorts out the score sheets and arranges new pairings.

TOURNAMENT TACTICS

Elimination events. Jumping off to an early lead should be your prime objective, for it gives you a degree of control over the doubling pace in succeeding games. Canny tournament players know this, and, as a result, you will find a good deal of bluffing with the doubling cube, particularly in the first game or two of the match. The inexperienced player in an unfamiliar setting, pitted against a confident opponent, is likely to play conservatively, declining playable doubles, and thus fall quickly behind.

After the first game or two the score becomes paramount. The player in the lead doubles more conservatively, since a change in the dice may bring forth a redouble or a gammon, suddenly dissipating his lead. Conversely, the player who trails generally doubles more freely in an effort to catch up.

Perhaps the best strategy against a more experienced player is to strike boldly, double aggressively, and accept most doubles. You may thereby be able to win the first game or two and put your opponent off stride. Given a little luck with the dice, you may take an early lead, but don't then lapse back into a wooden game. The expert will eat you up in the 1- and 2-unit games, for the longer the match, the more chance the dice will run even, so that his skill advantage will determine the issue. By forcing the match to fewer, higher-stake games, you have your best chance of upsetting the favorite.

Round-robin events. A similar strategy should be followed in round-robin events, but for a different reason. If you follow the precepts of this book—making only sound doubles and declining doubles when you have an unsound position—the best you can hope for is a string of victories worth 1 or 2 units each, perhaps augmented by a few worth 4. Inevitably, your score sheet will show a couple of 1-unit losses when you prudently declined a double. This will give you a very respectable win-loss percentage, but unfortunately, in most round-robin tournaments the winner is the player with the greatest number of points, not matches won. So you cannot afford to average 1 or 2 units a game, particularly since you will lose a game here and there. You must seek the large numbers, so get the doubling cube moving early. Chances are you will get some cooperation from the other side of the table, since most competitors look for action and many are familiar with this strategy.

Duplicate events. These are a recent novelty, rather than regularly scheduled events. Therefore there is no "book" on winning play. The best advice we can offer is to play soundly, since you are assured that the other players in your group cannot outroll you. Nonetheless, some lucky players may get better mileage than they deserve from their poor moves, so it is probably wise to loosen up your doubling tactics a bit.

GAMMONS IN TOURNAMENT PLAY

In all forms of tournament play, you should make a determined effort to get into gammon range, even at the risk of losing your advantage. A gammon is your only sure route to a 2-unit game, since your opponent may decline a double. When the cube has already been turned once or twice, the prospect of a gammon is particularly inviting and warrants some risk-taking. Remember you are looking for big numbers in round-robin play and against stronger opposition in elimination play. In duplicate events, an extra gammon or two will help offset the times your superior move somehow worked out badly.

MONEY GAMES

Most money games are head-to-head affairs lasting a few hours at least. The players have ample opportunity to study the tactics, strategy, and doubling pattern of their adversary. In long matches, knowledge of one's opponent counts for more than innate skill, so be sure to do your homework in the early games.

Look for flaws in your opponent's doubling habits, seek out his doubling threshold. Observe if he handles certain situations awkwardly—running his back men too soon or too late; leaving inopportune blots; in the end game, running when he should stay back, or *vice versa*. Once you spot such quirks, you can exploit your knowledge when the situation recurs. Double more quickly then, or accept his double when otherwise you might not. Play aggressively in these positions to bring additional pressure to bear.

The cardinal doubling rule applies doubly in money games; double whenever you think your opponent will decline. A sure win in a fraction of the time boosts one's ego and fills the wallet.

Psychology ranks with knowledge of the opponent's habits as crucial factors in a money game. Exude confidence, make your moves decisively, decline doubles cheerfully. Let your opponent sense that you expect to win in the long run. He may feel the pressure and fail to play up to his usual standard.

Play for any stake you can afford, else the money pressure may overwhelm your good judgment. And keep the stake constant, barring automatic doubles and the like. Remember that the patsy across the table may emerge in the late games as a canny hustler.

Do not let your opponent dictate the pace or style of the game. If he is behind and begins to double wildly and play recklessly, do not follow suit. Continue to evaluate each double dispassionately, play soundly, make aggressive moves only when you are trying to recoup a lost game or win a gammon.

When you fall behind in the score, do not try to get it back in a game or two. Try to forget the score and play each new game as if it were the first.

Take time out to kibitz other games, particularly when you are in a losing streak. Since you have no direct stake or participation in those games, you will be able to observe objectively and pick out winning mannerisms, moves, and doubling styles, and incorporate some of these features into your game.

Lastly, do not let your game go wooden. Play against many opponents, observe their approaches to situations, and never become so complacent that you cannot learn a new tactic.

SOCIAL GAMES

Avoid them!

Backgammon is by nature a gambling game, and if there is no stake, the game becomes sloppy and reckless. The stakes need not be high; play for a nickel a point if you wish, but play for something.

Backgammon is too great a game to be treated frivolously.

A BACKGAMMON BLESSING

> May the dice look with favor on you and the laws
> of probability treat you justly.
> May your opponents be worthy, granting
> you satisfaction in victory, earning
> praise in defeat.

Glossary

In addition to terms widely known to backgammon players, this glossary includes a number of terms coined by the author to simplify explanations. These are marked with an asterisk (*). Words defined elsewhere in the glossary are set in italics.

Automatic double—the practice of turning the *doubling cube* whenever the initial roll of the dice is a *double*. This is not allowed in tournament play.

Back game—the strategy of occupying two *points* in the opponent's *home board*, hoping for a *hit*, when one is far behind in the *running game*.

Backgammon—(1) a game in which one player has *borne off* all his men while his opponent's fifteen men remain in play, including at least one on the *bar* or in the opposing *home board*. The value of such a game is three times the figure on the *doubling cube*; (2) the name of a 5000-year-old game known as the King of Games and the Games of Kings, literally "back game" from the Middle English word *back gamen.*

Back men—the two men initially positioned farthest from one's *home board*, at the opponent's 1 point (B1).

Balanced board—an even distribution of men in one's *home board*, ensuring that two men will be *borne off* on the first roll or two.

Bar—the strip or band dividing the *home boards* from the *outer boards*, the temporary resting place for a man who has been *hit* before he reenters the game.

Bar point—the 7 *point* (coded W7 or B7 in this book), the first point outside the *home board.*

Bear off—to remove one's men according to rolls of the dice after they are all assembled in one's *home board.*

Beaver—in money games, the practice of allowing a player who is *doubled* to *redouble* immediately and to retain *control of the doubling cube.*

Blocked point—two or more men on a *point*, thereby securing it against a *hit*; usually shortened to *point.*

Blocking game—the strategy by which one hopes to construct a series of *blocked points* behind which an opposing man or men will be trapped.

Blot—a single man on a *point*, therefore vulnerable to be *hit*.

Blot-hitting contest—the situation where each player leaves men open to attack and takes almost every opportunity to *hit* them.

Box—the solitary player who plays against two or more opponents in the form of backgammon known as *chouette*. Also known as *man in the box*.

Breaking a prime—moving at least one man so that a *prime* no longer exists, almost always involuntarily.

Builder—a man available to combine with another to make a *blocked point*. He can be a *blot* or a surplus man on an existing blocked point (only two men are needed to secure a blocked point).

* **Building moves**—initial moves that send a *mid man* into one's *outer board* as builders to make a later *blocked point*. The conventional ones are 5-4, 5-2, 4-3, and 3-1

Bump—colloquial for *hit*: to land on a point occupied by one opposing man, thereby sending that man to the *bar*.

Captain—in *chouette*, the player who consults with his teammates but decides the moves himself, competing against a solitary opponent, known as the *man in the box*.

Chance—the possibility or probability of (1) a particular number or total showing on the dice or (2) improving one's position or winning the game.

Chouette—a form of backgammon in which two or more players, headed by a *captain*, compete against a solitary opponent, known as the *man in the box*.

Closed board—a position in which each of the six *points* in one's *home board* is occupied by two or more men, so that an opposing man on the *bar* cannot re-enter. A *prime* in the home board.

Cocked dice—dice that land on the rim, the *bar*, or one of the men. Such a roll is invalid and the dice must be thrown again.

Combinations—the number of ways in which two numbers can appear on one roll of two dice. (Technically, there is only one combination but two permutations for two specific numbers, e.g., 6-5. See *permutations*.)

Combination shot—the opportunity to *hit* an opposing man 7 or more spaces distant, requiring the correct total of the two dice.

Contact—a condition where a *hit* is possible, that is, where all of one player's men have not advanced past all of the other's.

Control of the cube—the advantage gained from being the only player allowed to *redouble* the value of the game, the result of having accepted the last previous *double*.

Counting the position—calculating which player is ahead by comparing the total spaces the men must travel before they are *borne off*.

Counting turns (or rolls)—calculating which player is ahead by comparing the number of turns each needs, under normal circumstances, to *bear off* all his men.

Covering a blot—moving a man to the same *point* occupied by a single man of the same color, thereby creating a *blocked point* secure from attack.

Direct shot—the opportunity to *hit* an opposing man 6 spaces or less distant, requiring the desired number on either of the dice.

Double—(1) a roll of the same number on both dice, which has the value of four dice with that number; (2) to double the value of a game by turning the *doubling cube.*

Double bump—a *hit* of two opposing men on one roll of the dice.

Doubling cube—the device that a player turns to a higher number in offering to *double* or *redouble* the value of a game. Its faces are numbered 2, 4, 8, 16, 32, and 64.

* **Doubling threshold**—the positional level beyond which a player generally declines a *double*; a psychological block rather than a realistic determination.

Dropping a blot—deliberately leaving a *blot,* generally at a strategic point, hoping to cover it later.

Duplicate tournament—an innovation whereby a director throws the dice and calls out the numbers, so that all the players move identical rolls.

Elimination tournament—the head-to-head method of tournament play in which the winner advances to the next round and the loser is eliminated or enters a consolation flight.

Expectancy—the probability of an event occurring at a specific time, computed according to its long-term mathematical projection.

Forced move—a roll of the dice that allows only one move because (1) a man is on the *bar,* (2) opposing *blocked points* eliminate all but one move, or (3) in *bearing off,* only one move is available.

Free move—a roll of the dice that permits a choice of moves.

Gaining a tempo—obtaining a positional or time advantage by slowing down the advance of one's men homeward or accelerating that of the opponent's men.

Gammon—a game in which one player has *borne off* all his men before his opponent has borne off one. The value of such a game is twice the figure on the *doubling cube.*

* **Gammon count**—a means of calculating the chances of a gammon.

Getting the count—see *counting the position.*

Hit—when one lands on a *point* occupied by one opposing man, thereby sending that man to the *bar*

Home board—the portion of the playing area from which men are *borne off,* after they are all assembled there. It contains six *points,* numbered 1 through 6.

* **Home men**—the five men initially positioned in one's *home board* on the 6 point (W6).

Hustler—one who plays a superior game of backgammon, conceals that fact, and seeks to win money from less talented players.

* **Interior men**—a player's men within his *home board.*

* **Interior move**—a move entirely within one's *home board.*

* **Interior points**—points within one's *home board.*

Lover's leap—the term applied to the beneficial initial roll of 6-5 which advances a *back man* safely to join his *mid men.*

Making a point—bringing two men together on a *point,* thereby safeguarding both from a *hit.*

Man in the box—the solitary player who plays against two or more opponents in the form of backgammon known as *chouette.* Usually shortened to *box.*

Men—the pieces or checkers that are moved and finally *borne off* according to throws of the dice. Each player begins with fifteen men.

* **Mid men**—the five men initially positioned at the opponent's 12 point (B12).

Negative probability—the mathematical approach to figuring the chances of a particular number appearing on successive rolls of the dice by multiplying together the odds of that number not appearing and deducting the resulting fraction from 1.

Nothing board—see *nothing game.*

Nothing game—the awkward position of having to move one's men onto the 1, 2, and possibly the 3 point while waiting for a *shot* in a *back game* situation.

* **Odd-man advantage**—the safety margin of having one less man to *bear off* than the projected number of rolls would optimally remove. For example, five rolls ordinarily will bear off ten men. With nine men, one roll of a die is not needed and can be wasted.

* **On the come**—the expectancy of a beneficial roll of the dice, based on the laws of probability, on which a *double* is offered.

Optional reroll—the practice of giving the first player the option of discarding his first roll and rolling again and turning the *doubling cube* once. This privilege is generally accorded the second player also. It is not allowed in tournament play.

* **Outer board**—the portion of the playing area adjoining the *home board.* Each player has an outer board, with points numbered 7 through 12.

* **Outer men**—the three men initially positioned in your *outer board* at your 8 point (W8).

Permutations—the number of ways two numbers can appear on one roll of two dice, giving weight to the sequence in which they are thrown. Thus 6-5 and 5-6 are two separate permutations but only one combination. See also *combinations*.

Pigeon—a colloquial term derived from bridge which describes the victim of a *hustler*.

Pip—one of the spots on a die.

Playable move—any legal move, excluding one that *touches down* or terminates on an adverse *blocked point* or one in the playing area while a man of the same color is trapped on the *bar*.

Point—(1) one of the twenty-four slim triangles on a backgammon board which can be occupied by the men; (2) two or more men on one of these triangles, securing it from attack. Also *blocked point*.

* **Point-makers (or point-making moves)**—initial moves that make a new and useful point. Conventionally 6-1, 5-3, 4-2, 3-1, and all six *doubles*.

Pointing on a blot—hitting a *blot* and making a *point* there on the same roll.

* **Point zero**—an imaginary point outside the opponent's *home board*, from which a player reckons the distance one of his men has traveled homeward; a man on the *bar* may be said to be at point zero.

Prime—a position in which a player has *blocked points* on six successive *points*, so that an opposing man behind them cannot advance past them.

Probability—the mathematical chance that a particular event will occur, usually expressed as a fraction, percentage, or decimal.

Redouble—to offer to *double* the value of a game by turning the *doubling cube* after the cube has previously been turned at least once.

Round-robin tournament—the method of tournament play in which each player competes in short matches against many others and none is eliminated.

Run—to advance a man homeward.

* **Run-and-build moves**—initial moves that advance a *back man* 6 spaces with the number on one die and bring in a *mid man* as a *builder* with the number on the other. Conventionally 6-3 and 6-2.

* **Runner**—a man being advanced homeward, generally through the opponent's *outer board*.

Running game—the stragegy of advancing one's men as quickly as possible homeward, as opposed to the *blocking game* or the *back game*.

* **Running moves**—initial moves that advance a *back man* with the entire roll. Conventionally 6-5 and 6-4, occasionally 6-3 and 6-2.

* **Running points**—the count of spaces required to advance all of one's men to his *home board* and *bear* them all *off*, used in *counting the position.*

Securing a point—advancing a man to join a single man of the same color, thereby creating a *blocked point.*

Sending to the bar—hitting a single opposing man who must then go to the *bar.*

Settlement—an agreement to terminate a game at a value agreed to by both players.

Shot—an opportunity to *hit a blot* when he is within striking distance of an opposing man. (As opposed to hit—when a man is actually moved to hit the blot.) See also *combination shot* and *direct shot.*

* **Split-and build-moves**—initial moves that advance a *back man* one space with the number of one die and bring in a *mid man* as a *builder* with the number on the other. Conventionally 5-1, 4-1, and 2-1.

Splitting—moving a man off a *blocked point*, usually applied to moving a *back man* exactly one space.

* **Straggler**—the last man to be brought to one's *home board*, generally encountering opposing men along the way. See also *trailer.*

Swiss tournament—the method of tournament play whereby players with equivalent scores are matched together after each round.

Tempo—a unit of time. More broadly, the pace at which one advances his men or the ability to alter that pace.

Touching down—putting a man down on a *point* temporarily after moving him the count on one die before moving him the count on the second die.

* **Trailer**—a man who trails his companions in the journey to the *home board.* See also *straggler.*

Turning the corner—moving from the opponent's *outer board* into one's own outer board, thereby changing direction.